Discussion Strategies

Beyond
Everyday Coversation

David Kehe
Peggy Dustin Kehe

Illustrations by Andrew Toos

PRO LINGUA **ASSOCIATES**

Pro Lingua Associates, Publishers
15 Elm Street
Brattleboro, Vermont 05301 USA
Office 802-257-7779
Orders 800-366-4775
Email prolingu@sover.net
SAN 216-0579

At Pro Lingua,
our objective is to foster an approach
to learning and teaching that we call
interplay, the interaction of language
learners and teachers with their materials,
with the language and culture,
and with each other in active, creative,
and productive play.

The topics in this book were gathered between 1990 and 1997 from
articles in a variety of newspapers: *The New York Times, The Los
Angeles Times, The Seattle Times, The Seattle Post-Intelligencer,
The Chicago Tribune, The European, The Observer, The Japan
Times, The Daily Yomiuri,* and *The Stevens Point (Wisconsin)
Journal.* All of the illustrations are by Andrew Toos except for the
cartoons used with news articles on pages 37, 50, 62, 115, 154, and
174 which are clip art from the *Art Explosion 250,000 Images*
collection © 1997 by Nova Development Corporation.

This book was designed and set by Arthur A. Burrows using
Century Schoolbook for the text and display type. The book was
printed and bound by BookCrafters of Fredericksburg, Virginia.

Printed in the United States of America.
First printing 1998. 3000 copies in print.

Introduction

These activities follow and build upon the strategic conversation skills of our intermediate-level book, *Conversation Strategies*. However, this text stands on its own and may easily be used for its own purpose: developing discussion skills. The activities in *Discussion Strategies* are designed to help high-intermediate to advanced level ESOL students develop the skills needed at high levels of communicative interaction.

From the early units on, students, in a step-by-step procedure, are given extensive practice in a variety of discussion strategies for leading and participating in a discussion. They are given focused practice with the following discussion techniques:

- using rejoinders
- asking follow-up questions
- seeking and giving clarification
- using comprehension checks
- answering with details
- soliciting more details from others
- interrupting others during a discussion
- recounting something they have heard
- volunteering an answer
- helping the leader of a discussion
- expressing an opinion
- referring to a source when giving an opinion
- leading a discussion themselves

Each unit builds on and recycles the strategies practiced in the previous ones, and for that reason, it is recommended that the class proceed through the book unit-by-unit in the given sequence. By the final units, students, while discussing sophisticated topics, are using all the strategies in large-group or whole-class situations.

Introduction

The general progression of interaction formats in the book is from participating with a partner in pair-work to leading large-group discussions. In the table of contents the inter-action formats are indicated as pairs, triads, small groups, and large groups or whole class.

In many of the units, summaries of newspaper articles are used as the topics for practicing the strategies and for carrying out the discussion. These articles have been cho-sen for their high-interest content. No article requires in-depth background knowledge, and the topics can be dis-cussed by students from any culture.

To students and teachers:
**All the articles in this book
are true stories.**

CONTENTS

General Structure of the Book

Discussion Strategies by Unit

The number followed by a letter – 67B, for example – indicates the page number and Student A, B, C, D, or E.

Contents

Contents

Contents

Editor's Pronouncement on Pronouns

In this book, we at Pro Lingua Associates are offering a solution to the vexing "he/she" pronoun problem. We have come to the conclusion that when a reference is made to a third person singular person, and that person is indefinite (and hence gender is unknown or unimportant), we will use the third person plural forms, *they, them, their(s)*. We are fully aware that historically these forms represent grammatical plurality. However, there are clear instances in the English language where the third person plural form is used to refer to a preceding indefinite, grammatically singular pronoun. Examples:

> Everyone says this, don't **they**?
> Nobody agrees with us, but we will ignore **them**.

If you will accept the examples above, it is not a major step to find the following acceptable:

> The learner of English should find this easier
> because **they** can avoid the confusion of using *he* or *she*
> arbitrarily, the awkwardness of *he or she, she/he,*
> or the unpronounceable *s/he,* and the implicit sexism
> of using *he* for everybody.

So in this book, you will find instructions such as, *Have your partner listen to the reading.* ***They** will interrupt you with clarification questions.* The reader of our text may disagree with our solution, but we ask **them** to blame us, the publishers, not the author.

Languages do change, and the English language needs to change its usage of gender-marked pronouns when they are clearly inappropriate. This is our solution, and we encourage you to try it out. And we invite your comments.

RCC for PLA

Discussion
Strategies

A Note of the General Structure of the Book

All of the activities in this book are for discussion groups. The first twenty-eight units, those which introduce and provide controlled practice of the discussion strategies, are for groups of two to five students. Units twenty-nine through thirty-eight, starting on page 191, give the students an opportunity to use their new strategies in less structured discussions; they involve large groups or the whole class in open discussion of the articles provided.

For the first twenty-eight units, each student has information not to be shared with with other students except as part of the discussion activity. To help make this clear to the students, they are called Students A and B in pair activities, A, B, and C in triad activities, etc. And the book is divided into sections, the first for Student A, the next for Student B starting in page 67, and the third for Student C (and where appropriate Students D and E) starting on page 133. These sections can be found easily using the black tabs marked AAA, BBB, and CCC, as you can see on the facing page. For example, Unit 1 begins on page 1 for A, page 67 for B, and page 133 for C.

We don't want anyone to get lost, so let's be sure everyone is on the right page and the start off with Unit 1. Have fun.

Rejoinders

I see.
Oh, yeah?
Really?
That's great!
That's too bad.

Follow-up Questions

(Questions about an answer)

A: **What did you do last night?**

B: **I watched a movie on TV.**

A: *(Rejoinder and Follow-up)* **I see.**
   <u>What</u> **movie did you watch?**

A
A
A
A
A
A

Format: Triads – Student B, page 67; Student C, page 133

Before the discussion
(1) *Silently* complete the questions below.
(2) Write two more questions about any topic.

Discussion Directions
(1) Ask *both* of your partners your discussion questions.
(2) After they answer, ask **follow-up questions** and use **rejoinders**.
(3) Take turns. You begin with discussion question #1. Student B asks #2, then Student C asks #3, and you continue.
(4) Answer your partners' questions *with details*.

Discussion Questions

1. Did you _____ yesterday?

4. When you were in high school, did you ever _____ ?

7. Have you ever _____?

10. What are some good points about _____ ?

13. Was anyone in your family ever a victim of a crime (e.g.,robbed by a thief)? *[Note: "e.g." is an academic abbreviation meaning "for example."]*

16. Which would you prefer to visit, a museum, a park, or a zoo?

19. _____ ?

22. _____ ?

Note: Follow-up questions frequently use WH-questions.

What movie?   Where did you see it?
Who was in it?   Why did you choose that one?
What did you think of it? How long was it?
How often do you go to the movies?

Rejoinders and Follow-up Questions   **• 1**

A
A
A
A
A
A

Clarification Expressions

Pardon?

Excuse me,
}}
{
What/Who/Where did you say _____ is?

Did you say _____?

You said _____, right?

You did what?

I'm afraid I didn't understand that.

Format: Pairs – Student B, page 68

Before Part 1 of the discussion

Without talking to your partner, fill in the blanks in Part 1.

Part 1 *Note: When two choices are given in parenthesies, choose one. Example, (yes/no)*

(1) Read your sentences to your partner and respond to their **clarification expressions.**

(2) Try to have a brief discussion about the topic in each sentence.

1. I'm planning to buy _____ this year.

2. Some day, I'd like to meet _____.

3. The movie I think you should see is _____.

4. _____ is a big problem.

5. Could you help me? I need help with _____.

6. _____ is one of the most interesting people in this school.

7. When I was a child, I spent a lot of time _____.

8. There are three things (my friend /I) really hate(s): _____.

9. If I had only one month left to live, I would _____.

10. (My friend / I) did something (funny / embarrassing) once. Here's what happened: _____.

Part 2

(1) Listen to your partner. Using **clarification expressions**, ask for clarification *after each sentence*, even if you understand clearly.

(2) After your partner answers, ask *follow-up questions* (see Unit 1) in order to have a brief discussion about the topic in each sentence.

1. *After sentence 1, ask:* Excuse me, you want to work in a *what* ?

2. You said you think computers are _____, right?

3-10. (Ask for **clarification** after each sentence.)

Clarification Questions, I
Comprehension Checks

(Do you) understand _____?
OK?   (Have you) got it?

Focus: Sentence-by-sentence clarifications with questions provided
Format: Pairs – Student B, page 69
Topics: Part 1. Flight Attendant Hero
             Part 2. Lost in a Jungle

Before Part 1 of the discussion
(1) *Silently* read your article in Part 1.
(2) Write answers to the *Factual Questions* about the article.

Part 1
(1) Read this article to your partner.
(2) *Stop after each sentence* and ask your **comprehension check.**
(3) In response, your partner will ask a **clarification question**.
(4) When you have finished all the sentences, ask your partner
     the *Factual Questions* and *Reaction Questions.*

Flight Attendant Hero

1. This article is about a 31-year-old flight attendant.
   Do you understand this first sentence?
2. The flight attendant works for British Airways.
   Understand sentence 2?
3. She was on a flight over the Atlantic Ocean on the way from
   London to New York.
   Do you understand this third sentence?
4. As the plane was flying over the ocean, the flight attendant
   looked out the window and saw some black smoke on the water.
   Got it?
5. It was very cloudy, but for about 20 seconds it was clear, so she was
   able to see the smoke.
   Understand sentence 5? *The article is continued on the next page.*

---

6. Flight attendants are trained to report anything unusual, so she told the pilot about the smoke on the water.
   OK?
7. The pilot turned on the emergency channel of his radio, and he could hear a signal from a fishing boat saying it needed help.
   Got the seventh sentence?
8. The pilot called the police in Boston, and they sent a ship to rescue the fishermen on the boat.
   OK?
9. Also, there was a helicopter in the area taking pictures of whales. They heard the pilot's call and rescued the fishermen.
   Do you understand what I just said?

Factual Questions about the article

Ask your partner the following questions.

1. What airline did the flight attendant work for?

   _____

2. Where was the plane flying to?

   _____

3. Was it a sunny day or a cloudy day?

   _____

4. What did the flight attendant see out the window?

   _____

5. What did the pilot do after the flight attendant told him about the smoke?

   _____

6. Who rescued the fishing boat?

   _____

Unit 3 is continued on the next page.

Unit 3, continued • Student A

Reaction Questions about your partner's opinions and experiences. Ask these questions and ask some follow-up questions.

A A A A A A

1. What airlines have you flown on?
2. When you fly in a plane, do you usually feel nervous?
3. Have you ever wanted to be a pilot or a flight attendant?
4. Have you ever seen an accident?
5. Have you ever gone swimming, fishing, or sailing on an ocean?

(You think of some *Reaction Questions* about this topic.)

6. _____
7. _____

Part 2
(1) Listen to your partner read a news article.
(2) *After each sentence*, your partner will ask a **comprehension check**. In response, ask one of the **clarification questions** below. There are nine sentences.
(3) Then answer the *Factual Questions* and *Reaction Questions*.

Clarification Questions

Lost in a Jungle

1. Did you say it took place in North America?
2. What did you say was in the middle of the rain forest?
3. What sickness did the uncle get? And could you spell it?
4. Why did they eat wild fruit?
5. Could you repeat that, please?
6. You said that there were snakes, crocodiles, and what?
7. Did the jaguar kill them?
8. I didn't understand that. Could you repeat it?
9. What did they have on their bodies?

Factual Questions about the article
Answer your partner's questions.

Reaction Questions about your opinions and experiences
Try to answer all your partner's questions and follow-up questions *with details*.

Clarification Questions, I • 5

Clarification Questions, II

Focus: Sentence-by-sentence clarifications, questions *not* provided
Format: Pairs – Student B, page 72
Topics: Part 1. Giant Baby
Part 2. Music, Reading, and Math

Before Part 1 of the discussion
(1) *Silently* read your article in Part 1.
(2) Write answers to the *Factual Questions* about the article.

Part 1
(1) Read this article to your partner.
(2) *Stop after each sentence* and ask your **comprehension check.**
(3) In response, your partner will ask a **clarification question.**
(4) When you have finished all the sentences, ask your partner the *Factual Questions* and *Reaction Questions.*

Giant Baby

1. There is a 17-month-old baby named Zack who is very large.
   Do you understand this first sentence?
2. Even though he is only a baby, he is about 1 meter tall and weighs 31 kilograms, which is about the size of an eight- or nine-year-old child.
   Did you understand that?
3. Because he is so large, he has to wear diapers that are adult size.
   Got it?
4. Also, he has to go barefoot because regular baby shoes don't fit him.
   OK?
5. Zack comes from a large family: his mother is 180 cm. tall and weighs 100 kilos; his father is 190 cm. tall.
   Do you understand what I just said?
6. Zack's mother was worried that he had a disease that made him so large, so his doctors did some special tests, but they found no physical problems.
   Understand?

This newspaper story is continued on the next page.

---

7. His mother is also worried because sometimes people are cruel to people who are different.
>   **Got it?**

8. People often stare at Zack when he goes shopping with his mother, but, except for that, people have been very kind and helpful.
>   **OK?**

9. Recently, some people gave Zack's parents an extra-large stroller for him and a special seat to use in the car.
>   **Understand?**

A
A
A
A
A
A

Factual Questions about the article

Ask your partner the following questions.

1. How old is Zack? (a) 12 months (b) 17 months   (c) 24 months?
   _____

2. Is he bigger or smaller than most children who are his age?
   _____

3. What does he wear that's adult size?
   _____

4. Why does he go barefoot?
   _____

5. Who's taller, his mother or his father?
   _____

6. Why did the doctors do some special tests on Zack?
   _____

7. What do people do when they see Zack at the supermarket?
   _____

8. What did some people give Zack's parents?
   _____

Unit 4 is continued on the next page.

A
A
A
A
A
A

Reaction Questions about your partner's opinions and experiences. Ask these questions and ask follow-up questions.

Giant Baby

1. When you were a baby, were you bigger or smaller than average?
2. Who is the largest person in your family?
3. Do you like your size now? Do you wish you were bigger? Or smaller?
4. Describe the size of the person you would like to marry.
5. Would you like to have children some day?
6. Tell me about a baby you recently touched, held, or played with.
7. What do you think is the most difficult thing about babies?
8. Tell me about an experience you had when people stared at you.

Part 2

(1) Listen to your partner read a news article.
(2) *After each sentence*, your partner will ask a **comprehension check**. In response, ask a **clarification question.** Samples are given below. *Even if you understand clearly,* ask a clarification question for practice.

Sample Clarification Questions

Did you say _____?
Could you explain what a _____ is?
Why did _____?
How many _____?
Who/What/Where/When/Why did you say _____?
I'm afraid I didn't understand that. Could you repeat it?

Factual Questions about the article

Answer your partner's questions.

Reaction Questions about your opinions and experiences

Try to answer your partner's questions *with details*.

Answering with Details

Format: **Triads** – Student B, page 75; Student C, page 134

Before the discussion
  (1) *Silently* read and answer the questions below for yourself, but *do not write the answers*.
  (2) Write two more questions about any topic.

Discussion directions
  (1) Ask these questions of *both* of your partners.
  (2) After they answer, ask them follow-up questions.
  (3) Answer their questions *with details* by using **and, but, so, because,** or **two sentences** each time you answer.

Discussion Questions

Some Personal Questions

  1. Are you happy now?
  4. After getting married, what would cause you to divorce your spouse?
  7. Do you enjoy visiting museums?
 10. What is your opinion of *this* group's members?
 13. Do your parents treat you and your siblings equally?
 16. Do you trust most people?
 19. _____?
 22. _____?

Discussion

Discussion

Format: Triads – Student B, page 77; Student C, page 135
Topic: Your High School Days

Before the discussion

(1) *Silently* read the questions below, but ***do not write*** the answers.
(2) Write two more questions about the topic.

Discussion directions

(1) Ask these questions of *both* of your partners.
(2) After they answer, ask them **follow-up questions**, and use **rejoinders** (e.g. "I see," "That's too bad," or "That's great!").
(3) Also, answer your partners' questions *with details*.

Discussion Questions:

Your High School Days

1. How did you get to school every day?
4. How long did it take you to get to school every day?
7. Did you belong to any clubs? If so, how many days a week did you have club activities?
10. About how many close friends did you have?
13. Did your school allow students to have part-time jobs?
16. In general, were you satisfied with your school rules?
19. Tell me about your favorite teacher in those days.
22. Were your high school days happy or boring for you, in general?
25. How many people from your high school days do you still keep in contact with?
28. Did your school have many female teachers?
31. About how many hours a day did you study outside of school?
34. What is your happiest memory from your high school days?
37. _____
40. _____

Paragraph Clarifications, I

A
A
A
A
A
A

Focus: Paragraph-by-paragraph clarifications, with clarification questions provided

Format: Triads – Student B, page 78; Student C, page 137

Topic: Animals in Movies

Before Part 1 of the discussion

(1) *Silently* read your part (A) of the article about animals in movies in Part 1.

(2) Write the answers to the *Factual Questions* about the article in Part 4.

Part 1

(1) Read this first part of the story (A) to your partners.

(2) *Stop after each paragraph* to ask your **comprehension check.**

(3) Then answer your partners' **clarification questions.**

Animals in Movies (A)

1. Have you ever seen a movie in which an animal was hurt or killed? Do you think this was a cruel thing to do to an animal?

   Do you understand this first paragraph?

2. There is an organization called "The American Humane Society" (in other words, AHS). This organization makes sure no animals are hurt or killed in movies. Before AHS started, many animals were hurt or killed during movie-making.

   Any questions about paragraph 2?

3. The first time an animal was hurt in a movie happened in a cowboy movie in 1939. In that movie, a specially-trained actor rode his horse off a mountain cliff and jumped into a river. The actor was OK, but the horse died. Many people were angry about this, so, after that, the AHS became advisors to movie-makers.

   Understand paragraph 3?

Unit 7 is continued on the next page.

Parts 2 & 3

Listen to Students B & C tell their parts of the story. *After each paragraph*, ask the **appropriate clarification question** below.

PARAGRAPH 4: Can you explain what a "battle" is?
PARAGRAPH 5: I'm afraid I didn't understand what you said.
PARAGRAPH 6: Did you say elephants jumped out of the airplane? Were they killed?
PARAGRAPH 7: You said the animals feel stress. Why?
PARAGRAPH 8: How many fish did they need?
PARAGRAPH 9: Could you explain that again?

Part 4

Factual Questions about the story

Ask your partners the following questions.

1. What is the abbreviation (in other words, the initials) for "The American Humane Society"?

2. What is the job of the AHS?

3. What happened in the cowboy movie in 1939?

4. Why were people angry about this cowboy movie?

Reaction Questions about your partners' opinions and experiences. Ask these questions and ask follow-up questions.

You, Animals, and the Movies

1. Tell me about a movie you saw recently that had an animal in it.
4. Do you go to movies often?
7. What is your favorite type of movie? Action? Mystery? Romance? Horror?
10. (You think of some questions about this topic of movies and animals.)

Paragraph Clarifications, II

A
A
A
A
A
A

Focus: Paragraph-by-paragraph clarifications, clarification
questions *not* provided
Format: Triads – Student B, page 80; Student C, page 139
Topic: Sleep

Before Part 1 of the discussion
(1) *Silently* read your part (A) of the article about sleep in Part 1.
(2) Write the answers to the *Factual Questions* about the article.

Part 1
(1) Read this first part of the story to your partners.
(2) *Stop after each paragraph* to ask your **comprehension check.**
(3) Answer your partners' **clarification questions.**
(4) Then ask your partners your *Factual Questions.*

Sleep (A)

1. Researchers are studying sleep. Research shows that people
   generally have two sleepy times every day: first, in the afternoon,
   around 2 to 4 p.m., and then around 10 p.m. to midnight.
   Do you understand the first paragraph?
2. Do you understand the expression "a sleep-deprived person"? A
   sleep-deprived person is someone who doesn't get enough sleep;
   in other words, they need more sleep than they get. Research
   shows that a normal person will take 10 to 15 minutes to fall asleep,
   but a sleep-deprived person will fall asleep in 3 or 4 minutes.
   Understand?
3. If you get sleepy after eating a big dinner, or while listening to
   a speech or concert, or after drinking a little alcohol, then you are
   sleep-deprived. If you can't stay awake all day without drinking
   some coffee or tea, then you are probably sleep-deprived.
   Got it?

Unit 8 is continued on the next page.

Paragraph Clarifications, II

Factual Questions about the article

1. How many sleepy times are there every day for most people?

_____

2. What are the sleepy times?

_____

3. What does the expression "a sleep-deprived person" mean?

_____

4. How long does it take a normal person to fall asleep?

_____

5. How long does it take a sleep-deprived person to fall asleep?

_____

6. What are three habits that show that you are sleep-deprived?

_____

Parts 2 & 3

  (1) Listen to your partners read the rest of the article.
  (2) When they ask if you understand, ask your own
      clarification questions, *even if you understand clearly.*

Part 4
Reaction Questions about your partners' opinions and experiences. Ask these questions and ask follow-up questions.

Sleeping Habits

1. How many hour's sleep do you need to feel good?
4. How many hours a night did you sleep when you were in high school?
7. Do you usually sleep better if you've gotten exercise during the day?
10. If you only sleep two or three hours at night, do you have problems the next day? (For example, do you feel irritable or unfriendly?)
13. (Think of two more questions about **sleep** and ask your partners.)

Student A • Unit 9 ∽

Asking for More Details

A
A
A
A
A
A

Could you give me an example of _____?
What do you mean by _____?
Could you explain _____?
Could you tell me why/who/what _____?
I'd like to know more about _____.

Format: Triads – Student B, page 82; Student C, page 141

Before the discussion
Silently read the sentences below and fill in the blanks.

Discussion directions
(1) Read these sentences to your partners.
(2) Listen to your partners' sentences. **Ask them for more details**.

Discussion Starters

1. My best friend _____

4. If I could have one thing that would improve my life, it would be _____

7. The thing I'm most afraid of these days is _____

10. One thing I'd like to change about the world is _____

13. In my opinion, the students in this class _____

16. I once told a lie about _____

Discussion

Format: Triads – Student B, page 83; Student C, page 142
Topic: Stress

Before Part 1 of the discussion
  (1) *Silently* read your part (A) of the article about stress in Part 1.
  (2) Write answers to the *Factual Questions* and then write two
     more questions.

Part 1
  (1) Read this first part of the article (A) to your partners.
  (2) Answer any clarification questions they have.
  (3) Ask them your *Factual Questions*.

Stress (A)

This is an article about stress. According to research, people who are close to their friends and family tend to live longer than loners. **Do you understand "loners"?** And people who have had heart attacks will live longer if they have close friends and family members.

To get more information about stress, researchers studied 40 monkeys. First, they put the monkeys in 4 groups. **Understand?** Then they shifted 3 or 4 monkeys from one group to another. For monkeys, it is very stressful to join a new group. So researchers could study the effect of stress on the health of the monkeys. **Have you got that?** They found that some monkeys remained friendly with each other even in stressful situations. For example, the friendly monkeys touched each other, combed each other's hair, and sat near each other. **OK?** After 26 months, they found that the friendliest monkeys were the healthiest. Also, the monkeys who were aggressive and upset from stress had the poorest health. **Do you understand this first part?**

Unit 10 is continued on the next page.

The friendliest monkeys were the healthiest

Factual Questions about the article

1. Who lives longer, people with many friends, or loners?

   _____

2. How many groups of monkeys were there in the research project?

   _____

3. _____

   _____

4. _____

   _____

A A A A A A

Parts 2 & 3

(1) Listen to your partners read the second and third parts
   of the article.
(2) Ask clarification questions when you don't understand.
(3) Answer the *Factual Questions* they ask you.

Part 4

**Reaction Questions about your partners' opinions and
experiences.** Ask the questions below and ask follow-up questions. Also, answer your partners' questions with details.

Stress in Our Lives

1. Do you have a friend or family member that you feel very
   close to? Who?
4. If you feel stress, do you: (a) eat food and candy (b) talk to a
   friend (c) go shopping (d) do some exercises (e) drink alcohol
   (f) do meditation to clear your mind (g) other?

   (Think of two more *Reaction Questions*.)

THE CHILDHOOD HOME
MATCH THE HOUSE WITH THE FACE

Discussion

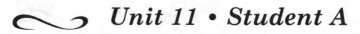

Discussion

Format: **Triads** – Student B, page 87; Student C, page 145
Topic: Your Hometown and Childhood Home

Before the discussion
   (1) *Silently* read the discussion questions below, but *do not write* the answers.
   (2) Write two more questions about the topic of your hometown and childhood home.

Discussion directions
   (1) Ask *both of* your partners your discussion questions.
   (2) Also, try to use these *discussion strategies*.

Discussion Strategies

Ask **follow-up questions** and **solicit more details.**
   (e.g., "Could you give me an example?" "What do you
   mean _____?" or "Could you explain _____?")
Use **rejoinders.**
   (e.g., "I see," "That's too bad," or "That's great!")
Answer questions **with details.**
   (e.g., answer with *and, but, so, because,* or with *two sentences*)

Discussion Questions

Your Hometown and Childhood Home

1. Where is your hometown?
4. When you were in junior high or high school, did you want to have a different hometown?
7. What is the weather like in your hometown in this season?
10. **Now let's talk about our childhood homes.** What was your favorite room in your childhood home?
13. Did you share your bedroom with anyone?
16. What view could you see outside your bedroom windows?
19. _____
22. _____

Discussion   **• 21**

Interrupting Someone

> **Excuse me. Could I ask something?**
> **Uhh, sorry for interrupting, but . . .**
> **Excuse me, but I have a question.**

Format: Triads – Student B, page 88; Student C, page 146
Topic: Telling Lies

Before Part 1 of the discussion
(1) **Silently** read your part (A) of the article about telling lies in Part 1.
(2) Write answers to your *Factual Questions* about the article .

Part 1
(1) Read this first part of the article (A) to your partners.
(2) ***Don't ask them if they understand***, but answer their clarification questions when they interrupt you.
(3) When you're finished, ask them your *Factual Questions*.

Telling Lies (A)

Most people would probably say that they hate it when someone lies to them. However, telling small lies, called fibs, is common. For example, have you ever told a friend that his or her hair style looks good, when actually, you thought it looked terrible? This is an example of a fib.

Researchers did a study on lying and found that lies are a part of everyday life. For instance, sometimes students will tell a lie in order to get a better grade, or a worker will tell the boss a lie in order to get a promotion. However, those are not the most common type of lies. More often, people lie in order to get other people to respect them. For example, let's say you exercise 4 days a week for about 40 minutes. If you want to impress a friend, you might tell him, "I exercise almost every day by jogging or by playing tennis for one hour." You didn't really tell the truth; you told this little lie because it made you feel good about yourself. This is the most common type of lie.

Unit 12 is continued on the next page.

Interrupting Someone

Factual Questions about the article

1. What are fibs?

   _____

2. What is an example of a fib?

   _____

3. When a worker tells a lie in order to get a promotion, is this the most common type of lie?

   _____

4. Why would someone lie to a friend about how many minutes they exercise?

   _____

5. Is lying to make you feel good about yourself a common or uncommon reason to lie?

   _____

Part 2

(1) Listen to Student B read the second part of the article.
(2) Interrupt *while* Student B is reading and ask **some clarification questions** *even if you understand clearly.*
(3) Try to use the **"Interrupting Someone"** expressions.

   For example: Excuse me. Could I ask something? What is the first type of lie called?

Part 3

   Listen to Student C, interrupt, and ask clarification questions.

   For example: Uhh, sorry for interrupting, but did you say introverts tell more lies?

Unit 12 is continued on the next page.

A
A
A
A
A
A

Part 4

Reaction Questions about your partners' opinions and experiences. Ask these questions and follow-up questions.

To Lie or Not to Lie

1. Let's say you're planning to go to a restaurant with your friend. Your friend says that he wants to eat at a Chinese restaurant, but you don't really want to eat there. If your friend said, "Is it OK with you if we eat at a Chinese restaurant?" would you tell the truth? Or would you lie and say, "Good idea. I want to eat there too"?

4. If someone asks you how much you weigh, do you tell the truth?

7. Tell me about a lie that you told your parents, a teacher, or a friend, when you were younger.

10. Do you think people in your country are usually honest or do they often tell polite lies? Give me some examples.

Words That Describe

Expressions

It is a person/animal/place/thing that ____.
It is an event/condition/situation that _____.
It is a type/kind/sort of ____.
You can find it at/in ____.

Format: Triads – Student B, page 91; Student C, page 149

Before starting
(1) *Silently* look at the words in the list below.
(2) *Do not show or tell your words to your partners.*

Directions
(1) Take turns. Using the expressions above, describe your
     words to your partners.
(2) Don't say the word.
(3) Your partners will try to guess the word.
(4) If they cannot guess the word, they can ask a question.

snake	crime	introvert	river
diapers	emergency	Nobel Prize	festival
stress	parachute	toy	a lie
	coeducational school		

Dropping a butter knife during a meal means a male visitor is forthcoming

Discussion

Format: Triads – Student B, page 93; Student C, page 151
Topic: Superstitions

Before Part 1 of the discussion
(1) *Silently* read your part of the article (A) in Part 1 below.
(2) Write answers to the *Factual Questions* and write two
    more questions.

Part 1
(1) Read this first part of the article to your partners.
(2) Then ask your *Factual Questions*.

Superstitions (A)

Galina is a 26-year-old Russian woman. When she gets out of
bed every morning, she tries to touch the floor with her right
foot first in order to avoid bad luck. If she had a bad dream
during the night, she will turn on the water in the bathroom
and retell the dream to the running water so that the bad
dream will disappear down the drain. Also, during a meal, if
she drops her butter knife, she believes she will have a male
visitor. If she puts on her sweater or shirt inside out, she takes
it off, throws it on the floor, and steps on it before putting it on
the right way. **Do you understand so far?**

Russians have always been very superstitious, especially about
important events such as marriage, death, and traveling. One
custom is called "sitting for the road." Before starting a trip,
everyone sits together for a moment in silence on their suit-
cases, a couch, or a bed. This custom is followed by traveling
businessmen, diplomats, and even cosmonauts. **Do you
know what a cosmonaut is?**

Unit 14 is continued on the next page.

A A A A A A

Factual Questions about the article

1. According to the Russian woman, which foot should touch the floor first in the morning?

   _____

2. What does the Russian woman do if she has a bad dream?

   _____

3. _____

4. _____

Parts 2 & 3

(1) Listen to your partners read the second and third parts of the article.

(2) Interrupt and ask clarification questions when you don't understand.

(3) Answer your partners' *Factual Questions*.

Part 4

Reaction Questions about your partners' opinions and experiences

(1) Ask these questions and then follow up-questions.

(2) Answer your partners' questions with details.

It's Your Lucky Day

1. What are some traditional things that people in your country do for *good* luck?

4. Do you have a lucky number?

(Think of two more *Reaction Questions* about superstitions.)

Telling What You've Heard

┌─── **Phrases for Telling** ───┐

A told me about . . . .
B said (that) . . . .
C told me (that) . . . .
B explained (that) . . . .
According to A, ...

Format: Triads – Student B, page 95; Student C, page 153
Topics: Part 1. Short People Live Longer
Part 2. Gossiping
Part 3. Why the French Have Fewer Heart Attacks

Before Part 1 of the discussion
(1) *Silently* read your article in Part 1.
(2) Write the answers to the *Factual Questions* about the article.

Part 1
(1) Tell Student B about your article, "Short People."
(2) Do *not* tell Student C.
(3) Student B will tell C what they heard about the article.
(4) Ask Student C your *Factual Questions* below.

Short People Live Longer

Researchers have found that short people seem to live longer than tall or heavy people. The researchers studied 400 men and found that shorter men lived about five years longer than taller men. Also, they found that smaller dogs, horses, and mice tend to live longer.

The researchers explained the reason for this. There are chemicals in the body called hormones. Certain hormones cause a person's body to become large. However, these same hormones also cause the body

This article is continued on the next page.

A
A
A
A
A
A

to get old faster. In a certain kind of very tiny mouse, they found that smaller individuals did *not* produce three types of hormones, or chemicals, that larger mice produce. As a result, the small mice of this species lived a year longer than the larger ones.

This research is especially important, because some doctors give special hormones to small children in order to help them grow larger. Unfortunately, these same hormones may cause the children to die younger.

Factual Questions about the article "Short People Live Longer"

1. Who lived longer: short or tall people?

2. Is this true or false? Smaller dogs live longer than bigger ones.

3. How many years longer did short men live than tall men?

4. What do we call the chemicals in our bodies that make us grow larger?

5. What do these same hormones also cause our bodies to do?

6. Which type of mouse had the three types of hormones: the large or small ones?

Part 2

(1) Leave your group and sit in a different part of the room. ***Do not listen*** to Student B's article.

(2) After Student B tells Student C about the article, come back to the group. Student C will explain the article to you.

(3) Answer Student B's *Factual Questions* about the article.

Unit 15 is continued on the next page.

Telling What You've Heard

Part 3

(1) Listen to Student C tell you about the article, "Vegetables and Wine." ***Don't take notes.***
(2) Tell Student B about the article.
(3) Student B will answer Student C's *Factual Questions* about the article. ***Don't answer or help.***

Part 4

Reaction Questions about your partners' opinions and experiences. Discussion about the article, "Short People Live Longer"

Your Feelings about Size

1. Are you happy with your height, or do you wish you were shorter or taller?
2. Are your family members tall, average, or short?
3. In general, have your relatives lived to an old age?
4. Do you think you will live to an old age?
5. If you had a child that was very short, would you ask a doctor to give them hormones to make them bigger?

Volunteering an Answer

┌ Phrases for Volunteering ┐

I think (that) . . .

In my opinion, . . .

I'd like to say (that) . . .

May I say (that) . . . ?

Can I answer that?

Can I respond to that?

Format: Small Groups – Student B, page 98; C, D, E 156-158

Directions for Asking

(1) Ask your questions below in any order.

(2) ***Do not ask anyone directly*** (i.e., don't look at anyone or say anyone's name).

[Note: "i.e." is an academic abbreviation meaning "that is" or "in other words."]

(3) Your partners will volunteer to answer.

Directions for Volunteering

(1) ***Volunteer to answer*** your partners' questions ***with details*** (answer with **and, but, so, because,** or **two sentences**).

(2) Try to answer first sometimes, and sometimes wait for your partners to volunteer.

(3) Ask follow-up questions, too.

Questions for volunteers to answer

• What time do you usually get up?

• What season is your birthday in?

• Have you ever smoked a cigarette?

• How many bedrooms are there in your house?

• How much money do you think you have with you right now?

• (You think of some questions.)

Discussion

Format: Triads – Student B, page 99; Student C, page 159
Topic: Divorce

Part 1

Pre-discussion
   (1) Before starting this discussion on divorce in Europe, ask
      your partners these questions.
   (2) Answer their questions.

1. This article is about divorce in Europe. Do you think divorce
   rates there are increasing or decreasing? What do you think is
   the reason for this?
4. Among European women, what do you think is the average age
   for marriage: (a) 18 (b) 23 (c) 25 (d) 28?

Part 2

Discussion Directions
   (1) Read the first part of the article to your partners.
   (2) Listen to Student B read the second part of the article.
   (3) Listen to Student C read the third part of the article.

DIVORCE (A)

The rate of European divorces has been increasing recently. This is especially true in the northern countries,
where the number of divorces rose between 1960 and 1992.

While the divorce rate increased in *all* the countries, it was
lower in countries that are traditionally Catholic. **Do you
understand "Catholic"?** For example, the divorce rate
was lower in Spain, Italy, Portugal, and Greece. On the
other hand, Britain, France, and the Scandinavian countries
had higher divorce rates. In fact, Britain had the highest
divorce rate, with one divorce in every three marriages.

This article is continued on the next page.

A
A
A
A
A
A

There are several reasons why divorce is increasing. First, women are becoming more financially independent. In other words, it is easier nowadays for them to find good-paying jobs, so they don't have to depend on husbands to support them. For example, in Scandinavia, where women are very independent, there tends to be a higher divorce rate. Second, many young people feel it is important to have a *romantic* relationship with their spouse. In other words, they expect to have a perfect marriage. However, if the marriage is not like their dreams, they start to look for a new and better spouse.

Part 3

Factual Questions about the article
Read the questions in *Part 1* to your partners again and try to answer their questions.

Part 4

Reaction Questions about your partners' opinions and experiences

Your Feelings about Marriage and Divorce

1. Is the divorce rate in your country increasing? If so, what are the reasons?
4. Do you think love is necessary in order to have a good marriage?
7. In your country, is it common for a couple to live together before marriage?

Clarifying by Summarizing, I

Focus: Summarizing (clarifications are provided)
Format: **Pairs** – Student B, page 102
Topics: Part 1. Getting Fat
                        Wrong Stadium
              Part 2. Bugs in Manila
                        Naked in the Laundromat

Before Part 1 of the discussion
(1) *Silently* read your two articles in Part 1.
(2) Write answers to the *Factual Questions* about the articles.

Part 1
(1) Read these two articles to your partner.
(2) *After each article,* answer your partner's **summary clarification questions**.
(3) Then ask your *Factual Questions* and *Reaction Questions*.

Getting Fat

I'm going to tell you about two articles. The first article is about Africa. There is a certain tribe in one country who thinks that fat people are beautiful. The men in this tribe think women are more attracted to fat men than to thin men, so many men try to become fatter. **Did you understand these first sentences?** Women think that if a man has a fat stomach, it means he is rich and can buy a lot of food. **Understand?** In fact, every October, the tribe has a contest to see who is the fattest man. To become fatter and to win the contest, one man lay in bed for 12 weeks and drank 19 liters of milk every day. **Did you get the third part?**

Unit 18 continues on the next page

Clarifying by Summarizing, I

A
A
A
A
A
A
A

Wrong Stadium

The second article is about two high schools in the U.S. They were scheduled to have a football game against each other. At the start of the game, an airplane was supposed to fly above the football stadium and two men were supposed to jump out of the plane and parachute onto the middle of the football field. **Did you understand this first part?** Unfortunately, the airplane pilot, who was a beginner, got lost. After a while, he saw a football stadium, so the men parachuted out of the plane. However, it was the wrong stadium. **Did you get the second part?** Some people in this wrong stadium, who were watching the football game there, thought the men coming down in parachutes were terrorists. Meanwhile, the people at the other game kept watching the sky and waiting for the airplane with the men in parachutes to arrive. **Understand?**

Unit 18 continues on the next page

Factual Questions about the articles

A
A
A
A
A
A

1. In the first article, where did the story about fat men take place?
_____

2. Why do the men try to become fatter?
_____
_____

3. What do women think when they see a fat man?
_____
_____

4. Why did that one man drink 19 liters of milk a day?
_____

5. In the second article, why did the men jump into the wrong stadium?
_____
_____

6. What did the people in the stadium think when they saw the men coming down in the parachutes?
_____

Reaction Questions about your partner's opinions and experiences. Ask these questions and ask follow-up questions.

Two Articles

1. Which do you think is more attractive, someone a little fat or someone a little skinny?
2. If you wanted to gain some weight, what would you do? What if you wanted to lose weight?
3. Tell me about a contest you or a family member has been in.
4. Which would you rather do, jump out of a plane with a parachute, climb a dangerous mountain, or go deep-sea diving with air tanks on your back?
5. When were you recently watching something as a member of an audience?

Unit 18 continues on the next page.

Part 2

(1) Listen to your partner read two articles.
(2) *After each article*, ask these **summary clarification questions**.
(3) Then answer your partner's *Factual Questions* and *Reaction Questions*.

Summary Clarification Questions

About the first article

1. I think you said that there is a problem in Manila because people are making fires and cooking roasts, right?
2. So if someone has a lot of cockroaches in their house, they can pay the police to kill the insects and they have to pay the police 10 cents for every dead cockroach?
3. In other words, a person with a roach farm can raise a lot of cockroaches and sell them to the government. Is that right?

About the second article

1. You said the man was alone in the laundromat because it was early in the morning, right?
2. I'm not sure if I understand. Did you say the man didn't want to take off his clothes because it was too cold, so he wore his wet clothes in the dryer?
3. I think you said the woman called the police when she saw the man. Did she call them because he was naked?

Factual Questions about your partner's articles

Answer your partner's questions.

Reaction Questions about your opinions and experiences

Try to answer your partner's questions *with details*.

Student A • Unit 19 ∽
Clarifying by Summarizing, II

Focus: Summarizing (clarifications are not provided)
Format: Triads – Student B, page 105; Student C, page 162
Topic: Catching Colds

Before Part 1 of the discussion
  (1) *Silently* read this first part of the article (A) in Part 1.
  (2) Write answers to the *Factual Questions* in Part 4.

Part 1
  (1) Read this first part of the article to your partners.
  (2) Answer their **summary clarification questions**.

Catching Colds (A)

In fall and winter, many people catch colds. In fact, colds are the most common reasons people miss work or school. People spend billions of dollars on cold medicines, but many people do not understand how we catch colds. **Did you understand this first paragraph?**

These are ways people do NOT catch colds: We don't catch colds because the weather suddenly changes or because cold air blows on us. Also, we do NOT catch colds because we didn't wear a hat when it was cold outside or because we went outside with a wet head. Also, we do NOT catch colds from too much work or from staying up late at night. **Understand?**

You may be surprised to learn that you can kiss someone with a cold and NOT have to worry that you'll catch it. Also, you do NOT have to worry if someone with a cold sneezes or coughs on you; in fact, we do NOT catch colds from people sneezing on us. **Got it?**

Unit 19 is continued on the next page.

Clarifying by Summarizing, II

Parts 2 & 3

   (1) Listen to your partners read the rest of the article on colds.

   (2) Ask **summary clarification questions** when asked if you
        understand, *even if you do understand clearly.*

   (3) Use the following expressions.

Summary Clarification Questions

Did you say _____?   **You mean** _____?

You said _____, **right?**   **In other words,** _____, **right?**

I think you said _____, **right?**

I'm not sure I understand. Did you say _____?

Part 4

Factual Questions about the article
  Ask these questions and answer your partners'.

  1. What's the most common reason people miss work or school?
      _____

  4. In winter, if you take a bath and then go outside with wet
      hair, will you probably catch a cold?
      _____

  7. If your brother has a cold and he sneezes on you, will you
      probably catch his cold?
      _____

**Reaction Questions about your partners' opinions and
experiences.** Ask these questions and then ask follow-up questions.

You and the Common Cold

  1. Before you heard the information in this article, how did you
     think people caught colds?

  4. What are some traditional cures for a cold in your country?

  7. What do you usually do to keep healthy?

Telling Other People's Opinions and Experiences

A
A
A
A
A
A

Format: Small Groups – B, page 107; C, page 164; D, page 166

Part 1
    (1) Discuss the *topics* below with your partners.
    (2) Try to give details and ask questions to get more details.
    (3) Listen closely to what your partners say, because in Part 2
        you will tell new groups what they said.

Discussion topics
    1. Tell us about a foreign country you've visited.
    5. Tell us about a terrible or an embarrassing experience you've
       had.

Expressions for Telling Others' Opinions and Experiences

I don't have an opinion about that,
        but I know someone who . . .
I haven't, but _____ has.
             (friend's name)

I've never done that, but my friend . . .
I'm not sure, but someone told me . . .
I don't know, but I do know someone who . . .

Part 2
    (1) Get into new groups.
    (2) Ask your new partners the questions below. Answer
        their questions by telling what you learned in your first
        group in Part 1. Use the expressions for "Telling Others'
        Opinions and Experiences."
    (3) ***Do not tell your own opinions or experiences***.
    (4) Ask questions to get more details.

Unit 20 continues on the next page.

Discussion questions
1. Have you visited any foreign countries?
5. Have you had any terrible or embarrassing experiences?

A
A
A
A
A
A

Part 3
(1) Discuss the *topics* below with your partners.
(2) Try to give details and ask questions to get more details.
(3) Listen closely to what your partners say, because in Part 4 you will form a new group and tell what they said.

More discussion topics
1. Tell us about a strange relative you have (e.g., a brother, uncle, or cousin).
5. Tell us about the most money you spent in one day or during one weekend.

Part 4

Directions
(1) Get into new groups again.
(2) Ask your new partners the questions below and answer their questions. Tell what you learned in your second group in Part 3. Use the expressions for "Telling Others' Opinions and Experiences."
(3) ***Do not give your own opinions or experiences***.
(4) Ask questions to get more details.

More discussion questions
1. Do you have any strange relatives?
5. Have you ever spent a lot of money in one day or during a weekend?

Discussion

Format: **Triads** – Student B, page 109; Student C, page 168
Topic: Driving

Before Part 1 of the discussion
   (1) *Silently* read your article about driving in Part 1.
   (2) Write answers to your *Factual Questions* and write two
       more questions.
   (3) Write two more *Reaction Questions* in Part 4.

Part 1
   (1) Read this first article to your partners.
   (2) Then ask your *Factual Questions*.

Driver
Goes to Prison

A driver who was drunk hit another car with his pickup
truck and killed two college students. This accident
happened in North Carolina, where the law says a
drunk driver can be punished by death if they kill someone. Lawyers wanted the driver to get the death penalty because they wanted to make him an example for
other people who might try to drive after drinking. In
other words, people might not drink and drive if they
know they could get the death penalty. In the end,
the drunk driver was sentenced to spend the rest of his
life in prison.

Unit 21 is continued on the next page.

                                                                          Discussion

Factual Questions about your article
Ask your partners these questions.

A
A
A
A
A
A

1. What was the drunk man driving?

_____

2. How many college students were killed?

_____

3. _____

4. _____

Parts 2 & 3

(1) Listen to your partners read the second and third articles.
(2) Interrupt to ask them clarification questions when you don't understand.
(3) Answer their *Factual Questions*.

Part 4

Reaction Questions about your partners' opinions and experiences

Ask these reaction questions and some follow-up questions. Write two more questions to ask. Answer your partners' questions with details.

Dealing with Drunk Drivers

1. How do you think drunk drivers should be punished if they kill someone while driving?
2. Does your country have strict rules about drivers who drink?
3. _____
4. _____

Helping the Discussion Leader Explain, I

Format: Triads – Student B, page 112; Student C, page 171

```
┌──────────── Expressions ────────────┐
│                                      │
│   Could you help me explain that?    │
│   Do you know what I mean?           │
│                                      │
└──────────────────────────────────────┘
```

```
┌──────────────── Example ────────────────┐
│ A: When I got up this morning, I felt    │
│    irritable.                            │
│ B: What do you mean by "irritable"?      │
│ A (to Student C):  Could you help me     │
│    explain that?                         │
│ C (to Student B):  Sure.  He means he    │
│    was in a bad mood.                    │
│    He was cross, grumpy, and mad at the  │
│    world when he got up this morning.    │
└──────────────────────────────────────────┘
```

Part 1

(1) Read the following sentences to Student B.

(2) Student B will ask you to clarify, but **you don't clarify.**

(3) Ask Student C to help you explain the sentences. Try to have a brief discussion about the topic of each of these sentences.

1. (Student B) , do you go to the dentist every year?
   After Student B's clarification question:
   (Student C) , could you help me explain?

2. Last night I went to a restaurant with my friends, but I didn't have enough money to pay for my dinner. I was terribly embarrassed.

3. Which would be the worst way to die: to fall out of an airplane, to fall off a ship, or to get lost in the desert?

4. I'm very good with animals. In fact, I was able to teach my dog a lot of tricks.

5. When was the last time you were a passenger on a plane, train, or bus?

Unit 22 continues on the next page.

Part 2

(1) Student B will read some sentences to Student C.

(2) Student C will ask Student B clarification questions.

(3) Student B will ask you to help clarify for Student C. Help Student B explain. Try to have a brief discussion about the topic of each sentence.

Part 3

(1) _Student C_ will read some sentences to you.

(2) You ask Student C the five clarification questions below.

(3) Student C will ask Student B to help clarify the sentences for you.

1. _(Student C)_, what do you mean by the word "crime"?

2. I'm afraid I didn't understand what you said.

3. I don't understand the word "pre-teen."

4. What are "clubs"?

5. Can you give me some examples of "study habits"?

Helping the Discussion Leader Explain, I

Unit 23 • Student A
Helping the Discussion
Leader Explain, II

Format: **Triads** – Student B, page 114; Student C, page 173
Topic: Part 1. Fathers Who Live Longer
Part 2. Smoking and Aging
Part 3. Tasting Foods

Before Part 1 of the discussion
(1) *Silently* read your article about fathers who live longer in Part 1.
(2) Write answers to your *Factual Questions* and write two more questions.
(3) Write two more *Reaction Questions* in Part 4.

Part 1
(1) Read this article to your partners.
(2) Don't answer your partners' clarification questions.
(3) Ask a partner to help you explain.
(4) Try to use the **"Help the Leader" Expressions.**
(5) Ask your *Factual Questions*.

"Help the Leader" Expressions

Could you help me explain that?
Do you know what I mean?

Unit 23 continues on the next page.

A
A
A
A
A
A
A

Fathers Who Live Longer

Researchers have found that fathers who help with child care tend to live longer that fathers who don't. In this study, researchers analyzed humans and nine species of primates (monkeys and apes) to see how males and females shared parenting duties. They found that among primates in which parents equally shared the care of their children, the life-spans of the males and females were almost the same. But, in the species in which the males took almost no interest in child-raising, the females outlived the males by many years. **Understand?**

For instance, in chimpanzees, where the adult males do almost nothing for the children, researchers found that there are about three times more adult females than adult males. However, among mountain gorillas, where the fathers protect and play with their young, adult males and females live almost the same number of years. For humans, the researchers studied 200 years of families in Sweden. They found that women tended to live five percent to eight percent longer than men. **Could you understand?**

Finally, some South American monkeys are especially interesting. The adult males always carry the babies shortly after birth except when the mother is feeding them. These adult males actually live longer than the females. **Got it?**

Factual Questions about the article
  Ask these questions about the article.

1. In this study, who did the researchers analyze?

  _____

2. _____

3. _____

4. What did the article say about the South American monkey?

  _____

Parts 2 & 3
  (1) Listen to your partners read their articles.
  (2) For practice, ask **clarification questions**, *even if you understand clearly.*

Part 4

Reaction Questions about your partners' opinions and experiences

Child-raising Fathers

1. About this article, were you surprised to learn about the results? What do you think caused the fathers to live longer?

2. **To men**: In the future, if you have children, do you plan to be active in child caring?

  To women: In the future, if you have children, will you expect your husband to be active in child caring?

3. _____

4. _____

Discussion

A
A
A
A
A
A

Format: Triads – Student B, page 117; Student C, page 176
Topic: Gambling

Before Part 1 of the discussion
(1) *Silently* read your part of the article about gambling in Part 1.
(2) Write answers to your *Factual Questions* and write two more questions.

Part 1
(1) Read this first part of the article to your partners.
(2) Then ask them your *Factual Questions*.

Gambling (A)

There is an important expression that you need to understand before we can discuss this article. Do you understand the expression "compulsive gambler"? The word "compulsive" means that you feel a strong need to do something; in other words, you *cannot* stop yourself from doing something. It's like an addiction. For example, some people are compulsive shoppers; this means they go shopping whenever possible, even if they don't need anything. There are also compulsive chocolate-eaters, compulsive TV-watchers and compulsive gamblers.

Compulsive gamblers feel great energy and excitement when they gamble. They forget about their problems, pain, and boredom. They have fantasies about how wonderful their life will be after they win a lot of money. Even after they lose, their excitement continues and even increases, because they feel that, if they continue gambling, surely they will win soon.

Unit 24 continues on the next page.

Discussion

Factual Questions about the article

Ask these questions about the article.

A
A
A
A
A
A

1. _____

2. What do compulsive shoppers do?

   _____

   _____

3. What are some other types of compulsive habits?

   _____

   _____

4. _____

Parts 2 & 3

(1) Listen to Students B & C tell about the second and third parts of the article.

(2) Interrupt and ask clarification questions when you don't understand.

(3) Answer their *Factual Questions*.

Part 4

Reaction Questions about your partners' opinions and experiences. Ask the questions below and some follow-up questions. Answer your partners' questions with details.

Lady Luck and You

1. Have you ever gambled?

4. What do you do when you feel bored?

(Think of two more *Reaction Questions* about gambling.)

Expressing Opinions, I

Format: Pairs – Student B, page 120
Topic: Information from a Survey

Part 1: Survey
   (1) Ask five or more people these questions.
   (2) Mark their choices on the chart.

Question	Number	Question	Number
1. What is the best age for women to get married?		**6 Where is the best place to have a vacation?**	
a. 20 to 23 years old		a. at a beach resort	
b. 24 to 26 years old		b. at a mountain resort	
c. 27 years or older		c. in a famous city	
2. What do you think about watching TV?		**7. Do you feel uncomfortable around foreigners?**	
a. a waste of time		a. Yes	
b. a good use of time		b. No	
3. Do you have a serious problem at this time?		**8. What kind of movie do you prefer?**	
		a. comedy	
a. yes		b. mystery	
b. no		c. adventure	
4. Which is the better season?		**9. Do you drink coffee every day?**	
a. summer			
b. winter		a. yes	
5. What is your blood type?		b. no	
a. A		**10.What is the best sport to watch?**	
b. B		a. tennis	
c. AB		b. soccer	
d. O		c. basketball	
e. I don't know.		d. baseball	

Student A • Unit 25, continued

Before Part 2 of the discussion

Silently read the sentences in Part 3 and choose an answer.

Part 2

(1) Listen to your partner give some opinions.
(2) Referring to your survey, agree or disagree with your partner using the expressions below.
(3) Discuss your own opinions.

Expressions for Agreeing

That's a good point. I found that most people . . .
I agree. I learned that most people . . .
You've got it right. Most people in my survey . . .

Expressions for Disagreeing

I'm afraid I disagree. I found that most people . . .
Are you sure? Actually, I learned that most people . . .
It's interesting. I found something different. Most . . .

Part 3

(1) Read these sentences to your partner.
(2) Discuss your own opinions.

1. In my opinion, most people enjoy ____ during their free time.
   a. watching TV
   b. playing sports or exercising
   c. reading books or magazines
2. I feel sure most people think that ____ is the best place to study.
   a. the library
   b. their bedroom
   c. a lounge

Unit 25 continues on the next page.

Expressing Opinions, I

3. Don't you think most people ____ ?
   a. want to live in their hometown in the future
   b. want to live someplace other than their hometown
4. I feel most people think that the perfect number of children tohave would be ____ .
   a. none
   b. 1
   c. 2
   d. more than 2
5. I'd bet that most people ____ .
   a. have smoked a cigarette at least once.
   b. have never smoked a cigarette
6. I believe that most people ____ feel stress in this school.
   a. often
   b. sometimes
   c. rarely
7. I think most people ____ to get exercise every day.
   a. try
   b. don't try
8. I feel sure most people think that ____.
   a. married life is better than single life
   b. single life is better than married life
9. During their high school days, I feel sure that most people enjoyed ____ the most.
   a. math
   b. science
   c. languages
   d. history
10. I imagine most people ____ around strangers.
    a. feel shy
    b. don't feel shy

A
A
A
A
A
A

Student A • Unit 26

Expressing Opinions, II

Format: Small Groups – B, page 123; C, page 179; D, page 182

Topics: Part 1. The Rights of Mothers and Fathers
Part 2. Death Caused by Cigarettes
Part 3. Circus Animals
Part 4. 63-year-old Woman Has a Baby

Agreeing

That's a good point.

I totally agree with _____.

That's right.

Disagreeing

I'm afraid I disagree.

That's a good point, but . . .

Actually, I think . . .

Before Part 1 of the discussion

Silently read this article about the rights of mothers and fathers in Part 1.

Part 1

(1) Read your article to your partners.

(2) Then ask the *Factual* and *Reaction Questions*.

Unit 26 continues on the next page.

Expressing Opinions, II

A
A
A
A
A
A

The Rights of Mothers and Fathers

Three years ago, Gina entered Harvard University, in Boston, with a full scholarship. She planned to graduate from Harvard, go to law school, and become a lawyer. Unfortunately, in her second year she had to return to her hometown in California when she found out she had gotten pregnant during the previous summer. The father of her baby is her ex-boyfriend, Tommy, who lives in California.

Now her baby is ten months old, and Gina wants to return with her baby to Harvard to continue her studies. But Tommy, the father, doesn't want Gina to take the baby. He says the baby should stay with him in California because he could take care of the baby better than Gina could. Tommy has a job as a waiter and makes about $800 month. He says his parents (the baby's grandparents) could take care of the baby while he's working. At the same time, he says Gina would be too busy with her studies at Harvard to be a good mother. Because she has no relatives in Boston, the baby would have to spend a lot of time in daycare while Gina is in classes or studying.

Gina disagrees with Tommy. She says that, as the baby's mother, she could take better care of the baby than anyone else and that a baby needs its mother. She is confident that she could study *and* take care of the baby. Also, she says that the baby will have a better future if Gina can graduate from a famous university like Harvard and become a lawyer.

Factual Questions about the article

Ask these questions about the article.

1. Why does the father, Tommy, think that the baby should stay with him?
2. Why does the mother, Gina, think the baby should stay with her?

Reaction Questions about your partners' opinions. Ask these questions about the article. Agree or disagree with your partners. Express your own opinions as well.

Parenting

1. Who do you think could better take care of this baby?
2. What do you think this couple should do?

Parts 2, 3, & 4

(1) Listen to your partners read their articles.
(2) Answer and discuss their questions.

Referring to a Source

Format: Triads – Student B, page 126; Student C, page 185
Topic: Bullying

Student B, page 126; Student C, page 185

Referring to a Source

I read that _____.
I heard that _____.
According to an article I read, _____.
According to the newspaper, _____.

Before Part 1 of the discussion
(1) *Silently* read the information from the article about bullying.
(2) **Do** not **read this article to your partners.**

Bullying (A)

This article about bullying in school tells about some things
that bullies do to other kids, and it explains why some kids
are victims of bullying.

There are many things that bullies do to hurt other
kids. Often bullies hit their victim. Also, when
their victim is walking past the bully, the bully will
try to trip them. It is common for bullies to call other kids
names, for example, "You big fat pig," or give a cruel nick-
name to someone, for example, "witch." They pull other
kids' hair and take away their lunch money. It is also
common for bullies to ostracize someone; this means that
they don't let the victim join their group or they tell their
friends not to talk to the victim. This is called "the silent
treatment." Some bullies do other strange things like force

This article is continued on the next page.

A A A A A A

their victims to wear a dog collar, crawl on their knees, or eat insects. It was reported that one young bully pushed hot pins under the victim's fingernails.

Why do some kids become the victims of bullying? Often a bully chooses someone who is different from the other kids. This could be a child with a big nose, freckles, or red hair. Sometimes the child has an unusual accent. It is common for victims to be small and physically weak; however, a very tall kid can also become a victim. Some kids become victims because they're smart and others because they're not smart. For example, at one school, a girl became a victim because she answered a lot of questions in class, and a boy was bullied because he had an unusual hair-style. Many victims of bullying are shy. **Source: *Chicago Tribune***

Part 1
(1) Don't read this article to your partners.
(2) Instead, ask the following questions.
(3) After your partners answer, tell them what you have learned from the article. Don't read it to them.
(4) Try to use the expressions for **"Referring to a Source."**

Questions for your partners
1. What do you think are some things bullies do to their victims? In other words, what do bullies do to hurt other kids?
2. Why do you think some kids are victims of bullying? In other words, why do bullies choose to hurt some kids?

Parts 2 & 3

Answer your partners' questions by giving your opinion. You don't have to refer to a source.

Part 4

Discussion about your partners' opinions and experiences with bullying. Ask your partners these questions and answer their questions.

1. When you were younger, was bullying a problem in your schools?
4. If you had a younger sibling who was being bullied, what would you do?

Summary Discussion

A
A
A
A
A
A

Format: Triads – Student B, page 129; Student C, page 187
Topics: Part 1. Best Friends
Part 2. The Effects of Watching TV
Part 3. Spanking

Before Part 1 of the discussion
(1) Review the Discussion Strategies with your partner(s).
(2) First, fill in the blanks in the Summary box below by asking each other for examples.
(3) Then go back to the unit where the strategy is introduced to review other phrases and expressions.
(4) Then *silently* read your article in Part 1.

┌─ Discussion Strategies Summary ─┐

Rejoinders (Unit 1)	*I see.*
Follow-up Questions (Unit 1)	_____
Clarification Expressions (Unit 2)	_____
Comprehension Checks (Unit 3)	*Do you understand?*
Answering with Details (Unit 5)	_____
Interrupting (Unit 12)	_____
Words That Describe (Unit 13)	*It's a type/kind/sort of*
Telling What You've Heard (Unit 15)	_____
Volunteering an Answer (Unit 16)	_____
Summary Clarification	
Questions (Unit 19)	*You said ____, right?*
Telling Others' Opinions (Unit 20)	_____
Helping the Leader (Unit 22)	_____
Expressing Opinions (Unit 25)	*That's a good point, but I'm afraid I disagree.*
Referring to a Source (Unit 27)	_____

GUYS... WE'RE 10 YEARS OLD NOW,
I THINK IT'S TIME FOR A
COMMITMENT

Part 1

(1) Read this article to your partners.
(2) Then discuss it, using the strategies above.

A
A
A
A
A
A

Best Friends

This article tells about some things that researchers found out about children's best friends. First of all, they found out that having only one best friend is common among adults, but it isn't common among pre-school children. Pre-school children will often say they have two or three best friends. For these pre-school children, their best friends are simply the children they play with most. On the other hand, when children are about ten years old, they choose their best friends according to personality.

Researchers also found that the number of friends for boys and girls is different. It's common for girls of school age to have one best friend, but boys usually have several good friends. Even at two years old, boys have more friends than girls do. Girls like to talk about their thoughts and feelings with a friend, so often they spend more time in pairs. Boys, on the other hand, spend more time in big groups.

Parts 2 and 3

(1) Listen to Students B and C read their articles.
(2) Then discuss their articles with them, using discussion strategies.

Part 4

Discuss your discussion

(1) Did you use a lot of the strategies?
(2) Which ones did you use?
Which ones didn't you use? Why not?

Rejoinders

I see.
Oh, yeah?
Really?
That's great!
That's too bad.

Follow-up Questions

(Questions about an answer)

A: **What did you do last night?**

B: **I watched a movie on TV.**

A: *(Rejoinder and Follow-up)* **I see.**
What movie did you watch?

Format: Triads – Student A, page 1; Student C, page 133

Before the discussion
(1) *Silently* complete the questions below.
(2) Write two more questions about any topic.

Discussion Directions
(1) Ask *both* of your partners your discussion questions.
(2) After they answer, ask **follow-up questions** and use **rejoinders**.
(3) Take turns. Student A begins with question #1. You ask #2, then Student C asks #3, and you continue.
(4) Answer your partners' questions *with details*.

Discussion Questions

2. What time do you prefer to _____?

5. Do you have any _____?

8. Where have you _____ recently?

11. Were you a good student when you were young?

14. Which member of your family _____?

17. Are you _____?

20. _____?

23. _____?

Note: Follow-up questions frequently use WH-questions.
What movie?	Where did you see it?
Who was in it?	Why did you choose that one?
What did you think of it?	How long was it?
How often do you go to the movies?	

Student B • Unit 2 ⌒

──── Clarification Expressions ────

Pardon?
Excuse me. }{ **What/Who/Where did you say _____ is?**
Did you say _____?
You said _____, right?
You did what?
I'm afraid I didn't understand that.

Format: Pairs – Student A, page 2

Before Part 1 of the discussion
   Without talking to your partner, fill in the blanks in Part 2.

Part 1
   (1) Listen to your partner. Using **clarification expressions**, ask
       for clarification *after each sentence*, even if you understand clearly.
   (2) After your partner answers, ask *follow-up questions* (see Unit 1)
       in order to have a brief discussion about the topic in each sentence.

   1. *After sentence 1, ask:* Did you say that you're going to buy _____?
   2. Pardon? *Who* would you like to meet?
3-10. (Ask for **clarification** after each sentence.)

Part 2 *Note: When there are choices in parentheses, choose one. Example, (yes/no/maybe)*
   (1) Read your sentences to your partner and respond to their
       clarification expressions.
   (2) Try to have a brief discussion about the topic in each sentence.

   1. In the future, I want to work in a _____.
   2. I think computers are _____.
   3. This coming weekend, I think you should _____.
   4. If I could change one physical thing about myself, I'd change _____.
   5. My favorite _____ is _____.
   6. I have a secret to tell you. I heard that _____.
   7. If I were an author, I would write about _____.
   8. I would rather win (an Olympic gold medal/an Academy Award/
      a Nobel Prize) than win (an Olympic gold medal/an Academy
      Award/a Nobel Prize).
   9. (My friend /I) got angry because _____.
   10. I need some advice about _____. Could you advise me?

Clarification Expressions

Clarification Questions, I
Comprehension Checks

> (Do you) understand _____?
> OK?   (Have you) got it?

Focus: Sentence-by-sentence clarifications with questions provided
Format: Pairs – Student A, page 3
Topics: Part 1. Flight Attendant Hero
              Part 2. Lost in a Jungle

Before Part 1 of the discussion
(1) *Silently* read your article in Part 2.
(2) Write answers to the *Factual Questions* about the article.

Part 1
(1) Listen to your partner read a news article.
(2) *After each sentence*, your partner will ask a **comprehension check**. In response, ask one of the **clarification questions** below. There are nine sentences.
(3) Then answer the *Factual Questions* and *Reaction Questions*.

Clarification Questions

Flight Attendant Hero

1. Could you tell me what a "flight attendant" is?
2. Which airline?
3. Where was the plane going?
4. Could you repeat that, please?
5. Did you say it was cloudy or clear?
6. What did she tell the pilot?
7. I didn't understand that. Could you explain it?
8. Could you explain what the word "rescue" means?
9. Did you say the helicopter was taking pictures of fish?

Factual Questions about the article
Answer your partner's questions.

Reaction Questions about your opinions and experiences
Try to answer all your partner's questions and follow-up questions *with details.*

Unit 3 is continued on the next page.

Part 2

 (1) Read this article to your partner.

 (2) *Stop after each sentence* and ask your **comprehension check.**

 (3) In response, your partner will ask a **clarification question**.

 (4) When you have finished all the sentences, ask your partner the *Factual Questions* and *Reaction Questions.*

Lost in a Jungle

1. This story took place in the Amazon rain forest in South America.
 Do you understand this first sentence?

2. Two sisters, one 9 and the other 13, were going on a walking trip with their uncle; they were going from their home to his farm, which was in the middle of the rain forest. The uncle's farm was about 320 kilometers from their home.
 Understand this next part?

3. The uncle suddenly died from malaria, so the sisters had to walk back to their home through the rain forest by themselves.
 OK?

4. They hadn't brought any food with them, so they had to eat wild fruit and sometimes a fish.
 Do you understand this fourth part?

5. They had only one box of matches and they found some wax or gum from a certain tree. They used it to cook and to make candles for light.
 Do you understand what I just said?

6. In this forest, there were lots of snakes, crocodiles, and jaguars (a big cat).
 OK?

7. They had a frightening experience when a jaguar saw them and ran toward them; fortunately, they were able to climb a tree to escape.
 Understand this seventh part?

8. After 31 days in the forest someone saw them and saved them, but one sister was very sick because she drank dirty water from a river.
 Got it?

9. When they were found, the girls also had big red mosquito bites all over their bodies. Now, however, they're all right.
 Do you understand this last part?

Unit 3 is continued on the next page.

Factual Questions about the article

Ask your partner the following questions.

1. Where did this story take place?

   _____

2. Why were these girls in the rain forest alone?

   _____

3. What were some dangerous things in this forest?

   _____

4. How many days were they alone in this forest?

   _____

5. What kinds of food did they eat?

   _____

6. In the end, did the sisters have any health problems?

   _____

Reaction Questions about your partner's opinions and experiences. Ask these questions and ask *follow-up questions.*

1. Have you ever gotten lost, when you were either walking or driving somewhere?
2. Do you ever spend time hiking or camping in a forest?
3. What's the most dangerous thing that happened to you as a child?
4. Tell me about a scary or surprising experience you had with a sibling (your brother or sister) or with a friend.
5. What underdeveloped part of the world would you like to visit?

   (Think of some *Reaction Questions* about this topic.)

6. _____
7. _____

B
B
B
B
B
B

Clarification Questions, II

Focus: Sentence-by-sentence clarifications, questions *not* provided
Format: Pairs – Student A, page 6
Topics: Part 1. Giant Baby
Part 2. Music, Reading, and Math

Before Part 1 of the duscussion

(1) *Silently* read your article in Part 2.
(2) Write answers to the *Factual Questions* about the article.

Part 1

(1) Listen to your partner read a news article.
(2) *After each sentence*, your partner will ask a **comprehension check**. In response, ask a **clarification question.**
Samples are given below. *Even if you understand clearly,* ask a clarification question for practice.

B
B
B
B
B
B

Sample Clarification Questions

Did you say _____?
Could explain what a _____ is?
Why did _____?
How many _____?
Who/What/Where/When/Why did you say _____?
I'm afraid I didn't understand that. Could you repeat it?

Factual Questions about the article

Answer your partner's questions.

Reaction Questions about your opinions and experiences

Try to answer the questions *with details*.

Unit 4 is continued on the next page.

Part 2
  (1) Read this article to your partner.
  (2) *Stop after each sentence* and ask your comprehension check.
  (3) In response, your partner will ask a **clarification question**.
  (4) When you have finished all the sentences, ask your partner
      the *Factual Questions* and *Reaction Questions*.

Music, Reading, and Math

1. Researchers found that students can improve their reading and
   math scores by studying music.
       Do you understand this first sentence?
2. They found that there is a connection between math and music, so
   they said that parents should add music to their children's education.
       Understand?
3. In this research, they gave reading and math tests to 96 children
   between the ages of 4 and 6.
       Got it?
4. After that, the children were divided into 2 groups: one group got
   Music lessons every day and the other group didn't.
       OK?
5. The next year, they gave all the students the same reading and math
   tests again and compared their scores from the year before.
       Did you understand what I just said?
6. The researchers found that the students who had received the
   lessons in music improved a lot on the math and reading tests.
       Got it?
7. Some students who were below-average readers became average
   readers after getting the extra music lessons.
       Understand?
8. The researchers said they were not surprised at the results because
   many people who are good in music are also good in math. For
   example, Albert Einstein, who was a math genius, loved to play
   the violin.
       Did you understand that?

B
B
B
B
B
B

Unit 4 is continued on the next page

Factual Questions about the article
Ask your partner the following questions.

1. What skills improved after studying music?

_____

2. How many children were in the study? (a) 76 (b) 96 (c) 106
   (d) 126

_____

3. Were the children teenagers?

_____

4. What types of lessons did half of the children get?

_____

5. When did they give the children reading and math tests?

_____

6. Which students' scores improved a lot?

_____

7. Were the researchers surprised?

_____

8. What instrument did Albert Einstein love to play?

_____

B
B
B
B
B
B

Reaction Questions about your partner's opinions and experiences. Ask these questions and ask follow-up questions.

Music, Reading, and Math

1. Were you surprised to hear about the results of this research?
2. Did your parents encourage you to study music when you were a child?
3. Did you like school when you were a child?
4. Are you good in math?
5. What musical instrument would you like to be able to play very well?
6. During what part of the day do you like to listen to music?
7. What types of things did you like to read when you were a child?
8. Nowadays, how many hours a day do you spend reading?

Answering with Details

Format: Triads – Student A, page 9; Student C, page 134

Before the discussion
(1) *Silently* read and answer the questions below for yourself, but *do not write the answers*.
(2) Write two more questions about any topic.

Discussion directions
(1) Ask these questions of *both* of your partners.
(2) After they answer, ask them follow-up questions.
(3) Answer their questions *with details* by using *and, but, so, because,* or **two sentences** each time you answer.

Discussion Questions
Some Personal Questions

2. What is the most challenging thing about learning English?

5. Which would you prefer to be: a) very smart b) very athletic
c) very artistic?

8. Are you interested in politics?

11. Are you a competitive-type person?

14. Is your best friend a male or a female?

17. How do you feel about horses?

20. _____?

23. _____?

B
B
B
B
B
B

Discussion

Discussion

Format: Triads – Student A, page 11; Student C, page 135
Topic: Your High School Days

Before the discussion
(1) *Silently* read the questions below, but *do not write* the answers.
(2) Write two more questions about the topic.

Discussion directions
(1) Ask these questions of *both* of your partners.
(2) After they answer, ask them **follow-up questions**, and use **rejoinders** (e.g., "I see," "That's too bad," or "That's great!").
(3) Also, answer your partners' questions *with details*.

Discussion Questions

Your High School Days

2. Where was your high school (e.g., in the countryside or in the middle of a city)?
5. What type of clothes did you wear (e.g., did you wear a uniform)?
8. In general, did you spend your free time with other high school kids, or did you spend time alone?
11. What did you usually do after school?
14. Did you ever have a part-time job in those days?
17. In general, what kind of relationship did you have with your teachers (good, bad, or average)?
20. How were your grades in high school (good, average, or low)?
23. How many people were in your class?
26. Did you take any special trips with your classmates?
29. What subjects were you good at?
32. How many boyfriends (if you're a girl) or girlfriends (if you're a boy) did you have?
35. What kind of hair style did you have then?
38. _____
41. _____

B
B
B
B
B

Paragraph Clarifications, I

Focus: Paragraph-by-paragraph clarifications, with clarification
       questions provided
Format: Triads – Student A, page 12; Student C, page 137
Topic: Animals in Movies

Before Part 1 of the discussion

(1) *Silently* read your part (B) of the article about animals in
   movies in Part 1.
(2) Write the answers to the *Factual Questions* in Part 4.

Part 1

(1) Listen to Student A tell the first part of the story.
(2) *After each paragraph*, ask the appropriate **clarification
   question** below.

PARAGRAPH 1:   Are you talking about movies?
PARAGRAPH 2:   Can you tell me again what the AHS does?
PARAGRAPH 3:   Why did the cowboy jump off a cliff?

Part 2:

(1) Read this second part of the story (B) to your partners.
(2) *Stop after each paragraph* to ask your **comprehension check.**
(3) Then answer your partners' **clarification questions.**

B
B
B
B
B
B

Animals in Movies (B)

4. Let's continue with this story about animals in movies. Have
   you seen a movie in which a group of soldiers or cowboys is
   riding horses into a battle? Sometimes it looks as though the
   horses are shot and fall down. Actually, these horses are specially
   trained to fall down. They're never hurt when they do this.
     Do you understand the fourth paragraph?
5. Moviemakers also use another technique called "animal-tronics"
   technology. In this, they make electronic animals that look like
   real animals.
     Got it?

The article is continued on the next page.

Paragraph Clarifications, I

6. There's a movie in which elephants jump out of an airplane with parachutes. Actually, these were all electronic elephants that the audience saw floating down from the sky. They were *not* real elephants.
   Understand paragraph 6?

Part 3
(1) Listen to Student C tell the third part of the story.
(2) *After each paragraph*, ask the **appropriate clarification question** below.

PARAGRAPH 7: What does movie set mean?
PARAGRAPH 8: What did you say that the AHS did for the fish?
PARAGRAPH 9: I don't understand "cockroaches."

Part 4
Factual Questions about the story
Ask your partners the following questions.

5. In movies with soldiers or cowboys, what sometimes happens to horses?

6. Are these horses hurt whan they fall down? Why (not)?

7. What are "animal-tronics"?

8. In the movie with the elephants, what did the elephants do?

Reaction Questions about your partners' opinions and experiences. Ask these questions and ask follow-up questions.

You, Animals, and the Movies

2. Would you like to work with animals, for example, taking care of them or training them?
5. How much does a ticket to a movie cost in your country?
8. What movie have you seen recently?
11. (Think of some questions about movies and animals.)

B
B
B
B
B
B

Paragraph Clarifications, II

Focus: Paragraph-by-paragraph clarifications, clarification
    questions *not* provided
Format: Triads – Student A, page 14; Student C, page 139
Topic: Sleep

Before Part 1 of the discussion
  (1) *Silently* read your part (B) of the article about sleep in Part 2.
  (2) Write the answers to the *Factual Questions* about the article.

Part 1
  (1) Listen to your partner (A) read the first part of the article.
  (2) When they ask if you understand, ask **your own
      clarification questions,** *even if you understand clearly*.

Part 2
  (1) Read this first part of the story to your partners.
  (2) *Stop after each papagraph* to ask your **comprehension check.**
  (3) Answer your partners' **clarification questions.**
  (4) Then ask your partners your *Factual Questions*.

B
B
B
B
B
B

Sleep (B)

4. About 100 million Americans are sleep-deprived. This means
   they don't get enough sleep. Most people get only 7 hours of
   sleep each night, but they *need* 8 to 8 1/2 hours. If you're sleepy
   during the day, it means you're not sleeping enough at night.
   Do you understand that paragraph?

5. Here is some advice about good sleeping habits. First, you
   should try to sleep without interruptions. This means you should
   sleep for 8 hours straight. You should *not* sleep for 5 hours, get
   up and do something, and then go back to bed and sleep for 3
   more hours.
   OK?

The article is continued on the next page.

Paragraph Clarifications, II

6. Second, you should go to sleep at the same time every night and get up at the same time each morning. You should *not* need an alarm clock to wake you up. Many people have trouble going to sleep on Sunday nights because they sleep late Saturday and Sunday mornings. **Got it?**

Factual Questions about the article

1. How many million Americans are sleep-deprived: a) 10 b) 50 c) 100 d) 150? _____
2. Do most people get 8 hours of sleep every night? _____
3. How many hours do most people need?

_____

4. Is it good to sleep for 5 hours, get up and do something, and then sleep 3 more hours? _____
5. Why do some people have trouble falling asleep on Sunday nights?

_____

6. Should you need an alarm clock to wake you up?

_____

Part 3

(1) Listen to your partner (A) read the first part of the article.
(2) When they ask if you understand, ask your own **clarification questions,** *even if you understand clearly.*

Part 4
Reaction Questions about your partners' opinions and experiences. Ask these questions and ask follow-up questions.

Sleeping Habits

2. Usually, when you go to bed, do you fall asleep after 1 or 2 minutes or after 10 minutes?
5. Do you have trouble staying awake during your classes? How about in high school?
8. Is there a type of music that makes you feel sleepy or that you listen to before going to bed?
11. When you feel sleepy, what do you do to feel more awake?
14. (Think of two more questions about **sleep** and ask your partners.)

Paragraph Clarifications, II   • *81*

Student B • Unit 9 ∽

Asking for More Details

Could you give me an example of _____?
What do you mean _____?
Could you explain _____?
Could you tell me why/who/what _____?
I'd like to know more about _____.

Format: Triads – Student A, page 16; Student C, page 141

Before the discussion
   (1) *Silently* read the sentences below and fill in the blanks.

Discussion Directions
   (1) Read these sentences to your partners.
   (2) Listen to your partners' sentences. **Ask them for more details**.

Discussion Starters

   2. _____ makes me angry.

   5. When I'm at a party, I _____

   8. One thing I'd like to change about my childhood would be ___
   _____

   11. If I get married, I want my spouse to _____
   _____

   14. I wish _____
   were still alive today.

   17. _____ is the best time of day to _____
   _____

Asking for More Details

Discussion

Format: Triads – Student A, page 17; Student C, page 142
Topic: Stress

Before Part 1 of the discussion
   (1) *Silently* read your part (B) of the article about stress in Part 2.
   (2) Write answers to the *Factual Questions* after the article
      and then write two more questions.

Part 1
   (1) Listen to your partner (A) read the first part of the article.
   (2) Ask clarification questions when you don't understand.
   (3) Answer the *Factual Questions* your partner asks.

Part 2
   (1) Read this second part of the article (B) to your partners.
   (2) Answer any clarification questions they have.
   (3) Ask them your *Factual Questions*.

B
B
B
B
B

Stress (B)

Let's continue with the second part of the article. Researchers also studied 90 married couples (of people, not monkeys). First they took blood samples from the couples. **Do you understand "blood samples"?** Then they asked the couples to find the solution to a disagreement that they had. Some couples argued and had a fight. Other couples were friendly in their discussion. **Understand?** After 24 hours, the researchers took another blood sample from the couples. The blood of the couples who had fought had changed. The blood samples showed that their bodies' ability to fight sickness had become worse. In other words, their condition was weaker after the stress of fighting. **Got it?**

This article is continued on the next page.

> Researchers also studied stress among college students when they were taking exams. They found that students who had close friends and family members had better health after the stress of taking exams. **Do you understand?**

Factual Questions about the article

1. What kind of sample did they take from the married couples?

   _____

2. What did they tell the married couples to talk about?

   _____

3. _____

   _____

4. _____

   _____

Part 3

    (1) Listen to your partner (C) read the last part of the article.

    (2) Ask clarification questions when you don't understand.

    (3) Answer the Factual Questions your partner asks.

Part 4

Reaction Questions about your partners' opinions and experiences. Ask the questions below, and ask follow-up questions. Also, answer your partners' questions with details.

Stress in Our Lives

2. When you were in elementary or high school, did you feel stress? What caused it?

5. Do you prefer to spend time with the same friends, or do you like to meet new people? Why?

(Think of two more *Reaction Questions*.)

THE CHILDHOOD HOME
MATCH THE HOUSE WITH THE FACE

A. B. C. D. E. F.

Discussion

Discussion

Format: Triads – Student A, page 21; Student C, page 145
Topic: Your Hometown and Childhood Home

Before the discussion
   (1) *Silently* read the discussion questions below, but *do not write* the answers.
   (2) Write two more questions about the topic of your hometown and childhood home.

Discussion Directions
   (1) Ask *both of* your partners your discussion questions.
   (2) Try to use these *discussion strategies*.

Discussion Strategies

Ask **follow-up questions** and **solicit more details.**
   (e.g., "Could you give me an example?" "What do you mean_____?" or "Could you explain _____?")
Use **rejoinders**
   (e.g., "I see," "That's too bad," or "That's great!")
Answer questions **with details.**
   (e.g., answer with *and, but, so, because,* or with *two sentences.*)

B
B
B
B
B

Discussion Questions

Your Hometown and Childhood Home

2. What is your hometown famous for?

5. When you're older, do you want to live in your hometown?

8. What's the best season in your hometown?

11. How many hours a day did you usually spend in your kitchen?

14. Is there anything about your house that you did not like?

17. Was it generally noisy, or quiet, in your neighborhood?

20. _____

23. _____

Discussion

Interrupting Someone

Excuse me. Could I ask something?
Uhh, sorry for interrupting, but . . .
Excuse me, but I have a question.

Format: Triads – Student A, page 22; Student C, page 146
Topic: Telling Lies

Before Part 1 of the discussion
(1) **Silently** readyour part (B) of the article on telling lies in Part 2.
(2) Write answers to your *Factual Questions* about the article.

Part 1
(1) Listen to Student A read the first part of the article.
(2) Interrupt *while* Student A is reading and ask **some clarification questions** *even if you understand clearly*.
(3) Try to use the **"Interrupting Someone"** expressions.

For example: I'm sorry for interrupting, but I have a question. What kind of lies are called fibs?

Part 2
(1) Read this second part of the article (B) to your partners.
(2) ***Don't ask them if they understand***, but answer their clarification questions when they interrupt you.
(3) When you're finished, ask them your *Factual Questions*.

Telling Lies (B)

This is the second part of the article about telling lies. Researchers found that there are two types of lies. The first type is the "self-centered" lie. This is a lie that we tell to help ourselves or to make ourselves

This article is continued on the next page.

---

look important We also tell self-centered lies because we're embarrassed. For example, let's say you borrowed your friend's bicycle and you accidentally broke something on it. When you return the bike to your friend, you tell your friend that part of the bike was broken before you got it. This is a self-centered lie; you told it because you were embarrassed, or because you didn't want to pay for the repairs. In general, the self-centered lie is one of the most common types people tell.

The second type of lie is most common among women. It's called the "polite" lie. We tell this lie to make another person feel good. For example, let's say you hate snow and cold weather. One day there's a snowstorm in your town. You meet your friend who loves skiing, and she says, "Isn't this snow wonderful!" You answer by saying, "Yes, it's great," even though you think it's awful. This is an example of a "polite" lie.

B
B
B
B
B

Factual Questions about the article

1. Why do people tell self-centered lies?

2. Are self-centered lies uncommon?

3. What type of lie is most common among women?

4. Give me an example of a polite lie.

Unit 12 is continued on the next page.

Interrupting Someone

Part 3

Listen to Student C, interrupt, and ask clarification questions.

For example: Please, I'm sorry to interrupt, but what kind of people are called "introverts"?

Part 4

Reaction Questions about your partners' opinions and experiences. Ask these questions and follow-up questions.

To Lie or Not to Lie

2. Let's say you're at a store and you buy something. It costs $8. You give the sales clerk $10. The clerk gives you back $5 in change. Would you tell the clerk about the mistake?

5. Let's say you had some homework to do, but instead of doing it, you went to a movie with a friend. The next day at school, your teacher asks why you don't have your homework. Would you lie or tell the truth?

8. When you tell a lie, do you worry about getting caught?

11. In general, do you trust your friends to always tell you the truth, or do you think they sometimes lie to you?

Words That Describe

Expressions

It is a person/animal/place/thing that ____.

It is an event/condition/situation that _____.

It is a type/kind/sort of ____.

You can find it at/in ____.

Format: Triads – Student A, page 25; Student C, page 149

Before starting
(1) *Silently* look at the words in the list below.
(2) *Don't show or tell your words to your partners.*

Directions
(1) Take turns. Using the expressions above, describe your words to your partners.
(2) Don't say the word.
(3) Your partners will try to guess the word.
(4) If they can't guess the word, they can ask a question.

B
B
B
B
B

flight attendant	salary	computer
neighborhood	genius	helicopter
battle	cowboy	habit
caffeine	party	cliff

Dropping a butter knife during a meal means a male visitor is forthcoming

Discussion

Discussion

Format: Triads – Student A, page 27; Student C, page 151
Topic: Superstitions

Before Part 1 of the discussion
(1) *Silently* read your part of the article (B) in Part 2 below.
(2) Write answers to the *Factual Questions* and write two
    more questions.

Part 1
(1) Listen to Student A read the first part of the article.
(2) *Interrupt and ask clarification questions* when you don't
    understand.
(3) Answer your partner's *Factual Questions*.

Part 2
(1) Read this second part of the article to your partners.
(2) Then ask your *Factual Questions*.

Superstitions (B)

According to Russians, we will have bad luck if we whistle
indoors, celebrate a birthday in advance, or return something
that we borrowed at night. They also believe colors can be
lucky or unlucky. For example, yellow flowers are considered
sad and so unlucky. Also, red can be unlucky. Russians are
suspicious of someone with red hair, because there are very
few redheads in Russia. **OK so far?**

Some superstitions are connected to traditional religious beliefs.
For example, there was a belief that all travelers were guarded
by their own personal angel. If you started on a trip but had to
return home because you forgot something, your angel would
wait for you along the roadside where you turned around. So,
when you returned home, it was important that you looked

This article is continued on the next page.

in the mirror, stuck out your tongue, and made an ugly face in order to scare away any evil spirits in your house and to bring your angel back to you before you started off on your trip again. **OK?**

Factual Questions about the article

1. According to Russians, when is whistling bad luck?

   _____

2. How do Russians feel about people with red hair? Why do they feel this way?

   _____

3. _____

4. _____

Part 3
(1) Listen to Student C read the last part of the article.
(2) *Interrupt and ask clarification questions* when you don't understand.
(3) Answer your partner's *Factual Questions*.

Part 4

Reaction Questions about your partners' opinions and experiences

(1) Ask these questions and then follow-up questions.
(2) Answer your partners' questions with details.

It's Your Lucky Day

2. In your country what do people think causes *bad* luck?
5. Do you do anything for good luck before taking a test or playing a game?

(Think of two more *Reaction Questions* about superstitions.)

Telling What You've Heard

┌─── **Phrases for Telling** ───┐

A told me about . . . .
B said (that) . . . .
C told me (that) . . . .
B explained (that) . . . .
According to A, ...

└────────────────────────────┘

Format: Triads – Student A, page 29; Student C, page 153
Topics: Part 1. Short People Live Longer
Part 2. Gossiping
Part 3. Why the French Have Fewer Heart Attacks

Before Part 1 of the discussion
(1) *Silently* read your article in Part 2.
(2) Write the answers to the *Factual Questions* about the article.

Part 1
(1) Listen to Student A tell you about the article, "Short People Live Longer." **Don't take notes.**
(2) Tell Student C about the article.
(3) Student C will answer Student A's *Factual Questions* about the article. **Don't answer or help.**

Part 2
(1) Tell only Student C about your article, "Gossiping."
(2) Do **not** tell to Student A.
(3) Student C will tell A what they heard about the article.
(4) Ask Student A your *Factual Questions* below.

Unit 15 is continued on the next page.

B
B
B
B
B

Gossiping

This article is about gossiping. Do you understand what "gossip" is? In conversations, when people sometimes talk about other people's private lives, it is called gossiping. We often imagine older women telling gossip to each other; in other words, they tell personal information about other people.

Researchers analyzed girls and boys between the ages of 9 and 12 in order to learn if they gossip and what they gossip about. By the way, children between 9 and 12 are called "pre-teens". The researchers found that pre-teens spend 50% of their conversation time gossiping.

Girls often talked about boys that they were in love with. They also talked about boys that other girls loved. Boys, on the other hand, rarely talked about special girls they loved. But they did talk about girls in general.

There was some interesting information about pre-teens. Pairs of boys who were good friends gossiped less than boys who were not close friends. In other words, boys used gossip to become friends with someone new. Girls, on the other hand, used gossip mostly with their best friends. Girls spent much more time gossiping with close friends than with girls who were just acquaintances.

B
B
B
B
B
B

Factual Questions about the article, "Gossiping"

1. What word means "having conversations about other people's private lives"?

_____

2. How old are "pre-teens"?

_____

Continued on the next page.

Telling What You've Heard

3. How much of pre-teens' conversations was gossip? (a) 25% (b) 50% (c) 75% _____

4. What did girls often gossip about?

_____

5. Did boys talk about girls whom they were in love with?

_____

6. Who did boys most often gossip with?

_____

Part 3
(1) Leave your group and sit in a different part of the room. ***Do not listen*** to Student C's article.
(2) After Student C tells Student A about the article, come back to the group. Student A will explain the article to you.
(3) Answer Student C's *Factual Questions* about the article.

Part 4

Reaction Questions about your partners' opinions and experiences. Discussion about the article, "Gossiping"

Your Feelings about Gossip

6. Do people in your country gossip?
7. When you were a pre-teen, did you talk about boys or girls that you loved?
8. In general, when you were in junior high and high school, what types of things did you talk about with your friends?
9. When you were a pre-teen, did you have a few very close friends, or many friends who were not so close?
10. Nowadays, what types of things do you talk about with your friends?

B
B
B
B
B

Student B • Unit 16
Volunteering an Answer

┌─ **Phrases for Volunteering** ─┐

I think (that) . . .

In my opinion, . . .

I'd like to say (that) . . .

May I say (that) . . . ?

Can I answer that?

Can I respond to that?

Format: Small Groups – Student A, page 32; C, D, E 156-158

Directions for Asking

(1) Ask your questions below in any order.

(2) *Do not ask anyone directly* (i.e., don't look at anyone or say anyone's name).

   [Note: "i.e." is an academic abbreviation meaning "that is" or "in other words."]

(3) Your partners will volunteer to answer.

Directions for Volunteering

(1) *Volunteer to answer* your partners' questions *with details* (answer with **and, but, so, because,** or **two sentences**).

(2) Try to answer first sometimes, and sometimes wait for your partners to volunteer.

(3) Ask follow-up questions, too.

Questions for volunteers to answer

- Do you have any older brothers or sisters?
- Where and when do you remember staying in a hotel?
- Do you believe in ghosts?
- Which do you prefer, cats or dogs?
- If you had to change your name, what name would you want?
- (You think of some questions.)

Discussion

Format: Triads – Student A, page 33; Student C, page 159
Topic: Divorce

Part 1

Pre-discussion
  (1) Before starting this discussion about divorce in Europe, ask
      your partners these questions.
  (2) Answer their questions.

2. In Europe, where do you think, the divorce rate is higher: in north-
    ern countries like Sweden, or in southern countries like Italy?
5. Among European men, what do you think is the average age for
    marriage: (a) 22 (b) 24 c) 26 (d) 28?

Part 2

Discussion Directions
  (1) Listen to Student A read the first part of the article.
  (2) Read your part of the article to your partners.
  (3) Listen to Student C read the third part of the article.

B
B
B
B
B

DIVORCE (B)

There is another interesting change in European marriage patterns. It is that many Europeans are getting married at a later age. The average age for women to get married for the first time is 25; for men, it's 28.

The increased divorce rate and the later age of marriage are having some interesting effects. In general, there are fewer children born nowadays, but there are more children born outside of marriage. In other words, nowadays, more children

This article is continued on the next page.

HEY! WHERE'S THE CANDLES?.. WE USED TO HAVE CANDLES EVERY NIGHT ... are you listening to me?

Many Young People feel it is important to have a Romantic Relationship...... They expect to have a perfect marriage

Discussion

are born to women who are not married. In Iceland, almost 60% of children are born outside of marriage. The reason for this might be that in Iceland, a Scandinavian country, women are more independent financially, so they can raise children by themselves.

In Italy, a Catholic country, only 7% of children are born outside of marriage. However, there are some interesting effects concerning birth rates in Italy. Because many couples are getting married at a later age, Italy's birth rate has dropped sharply. About 20 years ago, Italy had the highest birth rate in Europe; today, it has the lowest.

Part 3

Factual Questions about the article

Read the questions in Part 1 to your partners again and try to answer their questions.

Part 4

Reaction Questions about your partners' opinions and experiences

Your Feelings about Marriage and Divorce

2. Is it easy for women in your country to make enough money to survive if they get divorced?
5. If you wanted a divorce, do you think your parents would pressure you to stay married?
8. What would be your reasons for getting a divorce if you had no children? What would they be if you had children?:

Clarifying by Summarizing, I

Focus: Summarizing (clarifications are provided)
Format: **Pairs** – Student A, page 36
Topics: Part 1. Getting Fat   Part 2. Bugs in Manila
Wrong Stadium   Naked in the Laundromat

BeforePart 1 of the discussion

(1) *Silently* read your two articles in Part 2.
(2) Write answers to the *Factual Questions* about the article.

Part 1

(1) Listen to your partner read two articles.
(2) *After each article*, ask these **summary clarification questions**.
(3) Then answer your partner's *Factual Questions* and *Reaction Questions*.

Summary Clarification Questions

About the first article

1. You said this story happened in Africa and that the men in a certain tribe there think fat women are beautiful, right?
2. So, if a woman sees a fat man, she thinks he is rich?
3. You mean the man lay in bed for 12 weeks because he drank 19 liters of milk a day and got sick?

About the second article

1. Did you say there was a football game between two teams and an airplane was going to fly into the stadium?
2. In other words, the reason the pilot got lost was probably that he wasn't experienced, right?
3. I'm not sure I understand. You said some people watching the football game thought they saw terrorists. Why did they think they were terrorists?

Factual Questions about the article

Answer your partner's questions.

Reaction Questions about your opinions and experiences

Try to answer your partner's questions *with details*.

Part 2
  (1) Read these two articles to your partner.
  (2) *After each article,* answer your partner's **summary clarification questions**.
  (3) Then ask the *Factual Questions* and *Reaction Questions*.

Bugs in Manila

I also have two stories to tell you. The first story is about a problem in the Philippines. In the capital city, Manila, they have a lot of insects, for example flies and cockroaches, and they're having problems getting rid of them. **Did you understand the first part?** In order to stop the insects, the government is paying people to kill them. So if someone brings 10 flies to the police station, they will get 4 cents. If they bring in 10 cockroaches, the government will pay them 6 cents. **Did you get the second part?** Because people can make money killing insects, some people have secretly started to raise cockroaches. In other words, now there are roach farms. **Understand?**

B
B
B
B
B

Naked in the Laundromat

The second story happened in Canada. One day at about 4 a.m. a man went to a laundromat to wash the clothes that he was wearing. Because it was so early in the morning, nobody else was in the laundromat. **Understand the first part?** So the man took off all his clothes and put them in the washing machine. After he put all his clothes in the washer, he realized that it was very cold because he was naked. In other words, he had no clothes on. So, in order to get warm, he turned on one of

This news story continues on the next page.

Clarifying by Summarizing, I   • **103**

the clothes dryers and got inside of it. **Did you get the second part?** While he was in the dryer, he fell asleep. A little while later, another customer came into the laundromat to do her laundry. Suddenly she noticed the naked man in the drier. She thought he was dead. So she called the police and an ambulance. When they arrived they woke the naked man and everyone was surprised. **Understand?**

Factual Questions about the article

1. About the first article, what did the government pay people to do? Why? _____

   _____

2. Which could you get more money for: 10 flies or 10 cockroaches?

   _____

3. What are roach farms?

   _____

4. About the second story, why was the man the only person in the laundromat?_____

   _____

5. Why was the man naked?

   _____

6. What happened after the customer came into the laundromat?

   _____

   _____

Reaction Questions about your partner's opinions and experiences. Ask these questions and ask follow-up questions.

Two Articles

1. Do people in your country have problems with things like insects, mice, or snakes?
2. Do insects bother you a lot? Are you interested in them?
3. How often do you do laundry? What do you usually do while you wait to wash and dry your laundry?
4. Tell me about a time you stayed up until 4 a.m.
5. Tell me about a time the police talked to you.

Clarifying by Summarizing, I

Clarifying by Summarizing, II

Focus: Summarizing (clarifications are not provided)
Format: Triads – Student A, page 40; Student C, page 162
Topic: Catching Colds

Before Part 1 of the discussion
(1) *Silently* read this second part of the article (B) in Part 2.
(2) Write answers to the *Factual Questions* in Part 4.

Part 1
(1) Listen to Student A read the first part of the article on colds.
(2) Ask **summary clarification questions** when asked if
    you understand, *even if you do understand clearly.*
(3) Use the following expressions.

Summary Clarification Questions
Did you say _____?   You mean _____?

You said _____, right?   In other words, _____, right?

I think you said _____, right?

I'm not sure I understand. Did you say _____?

B
B
B
B
B
B

Part 2
(1) Read this middle part of the article to your partners.
(2) Answer their **summary clarification questions**.

Catching Colds (B)

How do people catch colds? We almost always catch a cold
because we touched something dirty with our hands and then
touched our nose, mouth, or eyes. Here's what usually
happens. A person has a cold. This person blows his nose and
gets cold germs on his hands. Then he touches something like
a telephone, door knob, book, or computer. After he touches
it with his dirty hands, a healthy person touches the same

This article is continued on the next page.

Clarifying by Summarizing, II   **• 105** thing and then touches his nose, mouth, or eyes. The germs enter our bodies in that way. **Did you get this first paragraph**?

You might be surprised to know that most people touch their nose, eyes, and mouth about three times an hour. So it's easy for germs to get inside our bodies. In order to keep from getting a cold, or in order to not give your cold to a friend, you should wash your hands often. **Understand?**

If you have a cold, you should use a paper tissue when you blow your nose, and then throw it away. Then, if possible, you should wash your hands before you touch anything like a book, pen, or telephone that other people will touch. If someone near you has a cold, you should try to wash your hands often and try not to touch your eyes, nose, or mouth. **Got it?**

Part 3
  (1) Listen to Student C read the rest of the article.
  (2) Using the expressions in Part 1, ask **summary clarification questions**, *even if you understand clearly.*

Part 4

Factual Questions about the article
  Ask these questions and answer your partners'.

2. We catch colds from touching certain parts of our bodies with dirty hands. What parts? _____

5. How does a person with a cold get germs on their hands? _____

8. If you don't want to get a cold from someone, what should you do often? _____

Reaction Questions about your partners' opinions and experiences. Ask these questions and ask follow-up questions.

You and the Common Cold

2. After you catch a cold, what do you do to get healthy again?
5. Tell about a time you were in a hospital.
8. Do you know anyone with bad health?

Telling Other People's Opinions and Experiences

Format: Small Groups – A, page 42; C, page 164; D, page 166

Part 1
(1) Discuss the *topics* below with your partners.
(2) Try to give details and ask questions to get more details.
(3) Listen closely to what your partners say, because in Part 2
    you will tell new groups what they said.

Discussion topics
2. Tell us about a prize you won. Was it for sports, or in a
   contest, or at a festival?
6. Tell us about a place in your country that we should visit..

Expressions for Telling Others' Opinions and Experiences

I have no opinion about that,
    but I know someone who . . .
I haven't, but _____ **has.**
        (friend's name)
I've never done that, but my friend . . .
I'm not sure, but someone told me . . .
I don't know, but I do know someone who . . .

Part 2
(1) Get into new groups.
(2) Ask your new partners the questions below. Answer
    their questions by telling what you learned in your first
    group in Part 1. Use the expressions for "Telling Others'
    Opinions and Experiences."
(3) ***Do not tell your own opinions or experiences***.
(4) Ask questions to get more details.

Unit 20 continues on the next page.

Discussion questions

2. Have you ever won a prize?
6. What place in your country should I visit?

Part 3

(1) Discuss the *topics* below with your partners.
(2) Try to give details and ask questions to get more details.
(3) Listen closely to what your partners say, because in Part 4 you will form a new group and tell what they said.

More discusion topics

2. Tell us about something you hate.
6. Tell us about a time when you were in a hospital or very sick.

Part 4

B
B
B
B
B
B

Directions

(1) Get into new groups again.
(2) Ask your new partners the questions below. Answer their questions by telling what you learned in your second group in Part 3. Use the expressions for "Telling Others' Opinions and Experiences."
(3) ***Do not give your own opinions or experiences***.
(4) Ask questions to get more details.

More discussion questions

2. Is there anything you really hate?
6. Were you ever in a hospital or very sick?

Discussion

Format: **Triads** – Student A, page 44; Student C, page 168
Topic: Driving

Before Part 1 of the discussion
(1) *Silently* read your article about driving in Part 2.
(2) Write answers to your *Factual Questions* and write two more questions.
(3) Write two more *Reaction Questions* in Part 4.

Part 1
(1) Listen to Student A read the first article.
(2) Interrupt to ask clarification questions when you don't understand.
(3) Answer their *Factual Questions*.

Part 2
(1) Read this second article to your partners.
(2) Then ask your *Factual Questions*.

Teenage Drivers

More teenagers die from traffic accidents than from any other cause. Many of the teenagers who died were passengers in cars driven by other teenagers; in fact, two out of every three teenagers who die in a car accident were in cars driven by another teenager! Because of this, there is a large organization that wants to change the way teenagers get driver's licenses. It recommends that all teenagers first get a *restricted* driver's license, which allows them to drive with a maximum of three

This article continues on the next page.

passengers and *only* during daylight hours. If, after driving with *a restricted* license for 18 months, a teenager has a perfect driving record (in other words, they have no tickets or accidents) and they are 18 years old, they can get a regular, *unrestricted* license.

Factual Questions about your article
Ask your partners these questions.

1. What's the most common cause of death for teenagers?
   _____

2. Is this sentence true or false? All teenagers who die in car accidents were in cars driven by other teenagers. _____
3. _____
4. _____

Part 3
   (1) Listen to Student C read the last article.
   (2) Interrupt to ask them clarification questions when you don't understand.
   (3) Answer the *Factual Questions*.

Part 4

Reaction Questions about your partners' opinions and experiences. Ask these reaction questions and some follow-up questions. Write two more questions to ask. Answer your partners' questions with details.

Driver's Licenses for Teenagers

5. Is it difficult to get a driver's license in your country?
6. Do you think it is a good idea to have a restricted driver's license for teenagers?

7. _____
8. _____

Discussion • *111*

Student B • Unit 22 ⌒◡◠⌒

Helping the Discussion Leader Explain, I

Format: Triads – Student A, page 47; Student C, page 171

Expressions

Could you help me explain that?
Do you know what I mean?

Example

A: When I got up this morning, I felt irritable.
B: What do you mean by "irritable"?
A (to Student C): Could you help me explain that?
C (to Student B): Sure. He means he was in a bad mood.
  He felt cross, grumpy, and mad at the world when he
  got up this morning.

B
B
B
B
B
B

Part 1
(1) Student A will read some sentences to you.
(2) You ask Student A the five clarification questions below.
(3) Student A will ask Student C to help clarify the sentences
     for you.

1. (Student A) , what's a dentist?

2. What do you mean by "embarrassed"?

3. Sorry. I couldn't understand the question.

4. Could you give me some examples of dog tricks?

5. What does "passenger" mean?

Unit 22 continues on the next page.

Part 2
(1) Read the following sentences to Student C.
(2) Student C will ask you to clarify, but **you don't clarify.**
(3) Ask Student A to help you explain the sentences. Try to have a brief discussion about the topic of each of these sentences.

1. <u>(Student C)</u>, do you know anyone who's a good athlete?
   After Student B's clarification question:
   <u>(Student A)</u>, do you know what I mean?

2. When I was younger, I always wanted my parents to get me a pet.

3. Usually, right before I take a trip abroad, I feel a lot of stress.

4. Do you think both spouses in a marriage should share the housework?

5. Have you ever felt homesick?

Part 3
(1) Student C will read some sentences to Student A.
(2) Student A will ask Student C clarification questions.
(3) Student C will ask you to help clarify for Student A. Help Student C explain. Try to have a brief discussion about the topic of each sentence.

B
B
B
B
B
B

Student B • Unit 23 ∽

<u>Helping the Discussion</u>
<u>Leader Explain, II</u>

Format: **Triads** – Student A, page 49; Student C, page 173
Topic: Part 1. Fathers Who Live Longer
         Part 2. Smoking and Aging
         Part 3. Tasting Foods

Before Part 1 of the discussion
   (1) *Silently* read your article about smoking and aging in Part 2.
   (2) Write answers to your *Factual Questions* and write two
       more questions.
   (3) Write two more *Reaction Questions* in Part 4.

Part 1
   (1) Listen to Student A read the first article.
   (2) For practice, ask **clarification questions**, *even if you
       understand clearly*.

Part 2
   (1) Read this article to your partners.
   (2) Don't answer your partners' clarification questions.
   (3) Ask a partner to help you explain.
   (4) Try to use the **"Help the Leader" Expressions.**
   (5) Ask your *Factual Questions*.

B B B B B B

"Help the Leader" Expressions

Could you help me explain that?
Do you know what I mean?

Unit 23 continues on the next page.

Smoking and Aging

This article discusses the effect that smoking has on people. Researchers were interested in finding out if smoking caused a person to age faster; in other words, if they look older faster. So they studied identical twins, because identical twins have the same genes; this means that they should age at the same rate, unless something on the outside causes one of them to age faster. **Understand?**

The researchers found 50 sets of twins in which one twin was a nonsmoker and the other a life-long smoker. They found that the smoking twin had skin that was 25% thinner than the nonsmoker. The reason that this is interesting is because thinner skin gets more wrinkles. As a result, the smoking twins had more wrinkles. **Did you understand that part?**

The researchers also found that there's a connection between smoking and gray hair and baldness. Surprisingly, 88% of smokers either were bald or had gray hair; on the other hand, only 68% of nonsmokers were bald or had gray hair. **OK?**

B
B
B
B
B

Unit 23 continues on the next page.

Factual Questions about the article
Ask these questions about the article.

1. _____

2. Why should identical twins age at the same rate?

   _____

3. Is this true or false? The nonsmokers had fewer wrinkles than the smokers.

   _____

   _____

4. _____

Part 3
(1) Listen to Student C read the last article.
(2) For practice, ask **clarification questions**, *even if you understand clearly.*

Part 4

Reaction Questions about your partners' opinions and experiences

5. About the article on smoking and aging, were you surprised to learn that people who smoke look older than people who don't smoke?
6. Do you know any pairs of twins? If so, do they look the same age?

7. _____

8. _____

Discussion

Format: Triads – Student A, page 52; Student C, page 176
Topic: Gambling

Before Part 1 of the discussion
(1) *Silently* read your part of the article about gambling in Part 2.
(2) Write answers to your *Factual Questions* and write two more questions.

Part 1
(1) Listen to Student A read the first part of this article.
(2) Interrupt to ask clarification questions when you don't understand.
(3) Answer their *Factual Questions*.

Part 2
(1) Read this second part of the article to your partners.
(2) Then ask them your *Factual Questions*.

B
B
B
B
B

Gambling (B)

Compulsive gambling is a psychological problem. Experts say that about 5% of the people who try to gamble lose control and develop serious problems. Most people who try to gamble and start to lose money understand that they should quit. However, when the compulsive gamblers start to lose, they decide to gamble more; they think the solution to their problem is to improve their gambling. Unfortunately, sometimes even average people can become compulsive gamblers.

Nowadays, many states in the U.S. have lotteries, and New York State has a typical one. In the New York lottery, a person can buy a ticket with six numbers on it for $1.00.

This article continues on the next page.

If some of the numbers are chosen, the person wins some money, but if all six of the numbers are chosen, it is possible to win a lot of money. Some lottery winners have won over a million dollars!

Factual Questions about your article
Ask your partners these questions.

1. _____

2. Is this true or false? When compulsive gamblers start to lose money, do they decide they should quit?

   _____

3. Please explain about the New York lottery.

   _____

4. _____

Part 3
(1) Listen to Student C read the last part of the article.
(2) Interrupt to ask clarification questions when you don't understand.
(3) Answer the *Factual Questions*.

Part 4

Reaction Questions about your partners' opinions and experiences. Ask the questions below and some follow-up questions. Answer your partners' questions with details.

Lady Luck and You

2. What things give you a lot of energy and excitement? For example: a. gambling   b. sports   c. music
   d. computer games   e. traveling   f. doing something dangerous, like driving a motorcycle fast   g. other

5. Do you sometimes have fantasies about being rich?

(Think of two more *Reaction Questions* about gambling.)

Discussion   • *119*

Expressing Opinions, I

Format: Pairs – Student A, page 55
Topic: Information from a Survey

Part 1: Survey
  (1) Ask five or more people these questions.
  (2) Mark their choices on the chart.

Question	Number	Question	Number
1. What do you most enjoy doing during free time?		**6. How often do you feel stress in this school?**	
a. watching TV		a. often	
b. playing sports or exercising		b. sometimes	
c. reading books or magazines		c. rarely	
2. Where is the best place to study?		**7. Do you try to get exercise every day?**	
a. library			
b. bedroom		a. Yes	
c. lounge		b. No	
3. Do you want to live in your hometown in the future?		**8. Which do you feel is better: married life or single life?**	
a. yes		a. married life	
b. no		b. single life	
4. What is the perfect number of children to have?		**9. In high school, which subject did you enjoy the most?**	
a. none		a. math	
b. 1		b. science	
c. 2		c. languages	
d. more than 2		d. history	
5. Have you smoked a cigarette at least once?		**10. Are you shy?**	
a. yes		a. yes	
b. no		b. no	

B
B
B
B
B
B

                                    Expressing Opinions, I

Before Part 2 of the discussion

Silently read the sentences in Part 2 and choose an answer.

Part 2

(1) Read these sentences to your partner.
(2) Discuss your opinions.

1. In my opinion, most people think women should get married at _____ years old.
   a. 20 – 23
   b. 24 – 26
   c. 27 or older
2. I think most people feel watching TV is _____.
   a. a waste of time
   b. an important use of time
3. I feel sure most people _____ a serious problem at this time.
   a. are having
   b. aren't having
4. I'd bet that most people _____ .
   a. like summer better than winter
   b. like winter better than summer
5. About blood types, don't you think most people would say ____?
   a. they have type A
   b. they have type B
   c. they have type AB
   d. they have type O
   e. they don't know what type they are
6. I believe most people like to vacation _____.
   a. at a beach resort
   b. at a mountain resort
   c. in a famous city
7. I think most people ____ uncomfortable around foreigners.
   a. feel
   b. don't feel

B
B
B
B
B
B

Unit 25 continues on the next page.

Expressing Opinions, I   • 121

8. Regarding movies, I think most people prefer to watch _____.
   a. comedy
   b. mystery
   c. adventure
9. I imagine most people _____ coffee every day.
   a. drink
   b. don't drink
10. I feel sure most people like to watch ____ .
    a. tennis
    b. soccer
    c. basketball
    d. baseball

Part 3
(1) Listen to your partner give some opinions.
(2) Referring to your survey, agree or disagree with your partner using the expressions below.
(3) Discuss your own opinions.

Expressions for Agreeing

Yes, you're right. I found that most people ...
I agree. I learned that most people ...
You've got it right. Most people in my survey ...

Expressions for Disagreeing

I'm afraid I disagree. I found that most people ...
Are you sure? Actually, I learned that most people ...
It's interesting. I found something different. Most ...

Expressing Opinions, I

Expressing Opinions, II

Format: Small Groups – A, page 58; C, page 179; D, page 182
Topics: Part 1. The Rights of Mothers and Fathers
Part 2. Death Caused by Cigarettes
Part 3. Circus Animals
Part 4. 63-year-old Woman Has a Baby

Agreeing

That's a good point.

I totally agree with _____.

That's right.

Disagreeing

I'm afraid I disagree.

That's a good point, but . . .

Actually, I think . . .

B
B
B
B
B

Before Part 1 of the discussion
Silently read this article about death and cigarettes
in Part 2.

Part 1
(1) Listen to Student A read the first article.
(2) Answer and discuss the questions.

Part 2
(1) Read your article to your partners.
(2) Then ask the *Factual* and *Reaction Questions.*

Unit 26 continues on the next page.

Death Caused by Cigarettes

Fifty years ago, when Jean Conner was a teenager, she started smoking cigarettes. She said she started smoking after seeing ads in magazines of beautiful models smoking and after watching famous movie stars smoking in movies. She thought smoking was glamorous. As she got older, she began to smoke more and more; soon she was smoking three packs a day. That means she smoked 60 cigarettes a day. At the age of 45, she quit smoking but a month later, she found out that she had cancer. She died four years later.

Now Jean Conner's daughter is suing the tobacco company; she wants the cigarette maker to pay her money because, she says, cigarettes caused her mother's death. According to the daughter, cigarettes are addictive, and cigarette companies try to make people start smoking and become addicted to tobacco. She also said that her mother started smoking before there were warnings on cigarette packs telling people that tobacco might cause health problems. She said cigarettes cause thousands of people to die every year.

This article is continued on the next page.

B
B
B
B
B
B

The tobacco company, on the other hand, says that they should not have to pay money to the daughter. The company says that people choose whether to smoke or not; cigarette companies don't force people to smoke. The company also says that even though Jean Conner knew there were health risks, she continued to smoke. Furthermore, the company said that Jean Conner was not addicted to cigarettes, because she was able to stop smoking at age 45 and 50 million other Americans have quit smoking, too.

B
B
B
B
B

Factual Questions about the article
Ask these questions about the article.

1. Why does the daughter think that the cigarette company should pay?
2. Why does the cigarette company think that it shouldn't have to pay?

Reaction Questions about your partners' opinions. Ask these questions about the article. Agree or disagree with your partners. Express your own opinions as well.

Curing the World of Cigarettes

1. Who do you agree with, the daughter or the tobacco company?
2. Do you think cigarettes should be illegal, like marijuana and other drugs? Would that stop people in your country and all over the world from smoking? What will stop them?

Parts 3 & 4

1. Listen to Students C & D read their articles.
2. Answer and discuss their questions.

Referring to a Source

Format: Triads – Student A, page 61; Student C, page 185
Topic: Bullying

Referring to a Source

I read that _____.
I heard that _____.
According to an article I read, _____.
According to the newspaper, _____.

Before Part 1 of the discussion
(1) *Silently* read the information from the article about bullying.
(2) **Do not read this article to your partners.**

Bullying (B)

This article about bullying explains why bullies pick on other kids, why they hurt other kids.

U sually, bullies are not aware of the feelings of others. They tend to think other kids are trying to annoy them or make them angry, even when they really aren't. Bullies feel that they have the right to react and hurt the other kids. Also, bullies usually have been victims of other bullies, so they learn to be violent from their own experience as victims; they believe aggression is the best solution to their problems.

Bullies also feel a great need to belong to a group. Bullies often have two or three friends who are also aggressive kids. They find that their friends admire physical

This article is continued on the next page.

---

strength, so one way for them to impress their friends is to pick on weaker kids. One girl said she bullied others because her friends did it, too. Another girl said she was afraid that if she didn't bully someone, her friends might bully her.

Finally, some kids bully others because they feel a kind of excitement when hurting others.
Source: Japan Times

Part 1
Answer Student A's questions by giving your opinions. You don't have to refer to a source.

Part 2
(1) Don't read this article to your partners.
(2) Instead, ask the following question.
(3) After your partners answer, tell them what you have learned from the article. Don't read it to them.
(4) Try to use the expressions for **"Referring to a Source."**

B
B
B
B
B
B

A question for your partners
Why do you think bullies pick on and hurt other kids?

Part 3
Answer Student C's questions by giving your opinions. You don't have to refer to a source.

Part 4
Discussion about your partners' opinions and experiences with bullying
Ask your partners these questions and answer their questions.

2. When you were younger, did you feel that you were different from other kids?
5. When you were younger, if someone was bullying you, how did you react?

Referring to a Source

Summary Discussion

Format: Triads – Student A, page 64; Student C, page 187
Topics: Part 1. Best Friends
Part 2. The Effects of Watching TV
Part 3. Spanking

Before Part 1 of the discussion
(1) Review the Discussion Strategies with your partner(s).
(2) First, fill in the blanks in the Summary box below by asking each other for examples.
(3) Then go back to the unit where the strategy is introduced to review other phrases and expressions.
(4) Then *silently* read your article in Part 1.

Discussion Strategies Summary

Rejoinders (Unit 1)	_____
Follow-up Questions (Unit 1)	*What movie did you see?*
Clarification Expressions (Unit 2)	_____
Comprehension Checks (Unit 3)	_____
Answering with Details (Unit 5)	*and, so, but, because*
Interrupting (Unit 12)	_____
Words That Describe (Unit 13)	_____
Telling What You've Heard (Unit 15)	*B said (that)* . . .
Volunteering an Answer (Unit 16)	_____
Summary Clarification Questions (Unit 19)	_____
Telling Others' Opinions (Unit 20)	*I know someone who.* . .
Helping the Leader (Unit 22)	_____
Expressing Opinions (Unit 25)	_____
Referring to a Source (Unit 27)	*According to* . . .

B
B
B
B
B
B

Part 1

(1) Listen to Student A read the first article.

(2) Then discuss it with your partners, using discussion strategies.

Part 2

(1) Read this article to your partners.

(2) Then discuss it, using the strategies above.

B
B
B
B
B

The Effects of Watching TV

This article tells about some problems that are caused by watching TV. There's a town in Canada that didn't have TV until only 20 years ago. Researchers compared the people in that town to people in two towns that had had TV for 40 years. They found that people who watch a lot of TV are not as creative as people who don't watch much. For example, the researchers gave some problem-solving tests to children. The children who didn't watch much TV had more ideas about how to solve the problems than children who watched a lot. They were also faster at thinking of ideas.

Researchers explained the reason why people who do not watch a lot of TV are more creative. To be creative, you need to become bored. When some people get bored, they just watch TV. They aren't active. When other people get bored, they start to think of ways to entertain them-selves. They become active and creative. For example,

This article is continued on the next page.

Summary Discussion

they play games, paint pictures, write letters, or go for a walk. Sometimes they seek out a friend to spend time with, a friend who enjoys socializing and doesn't want to watch TV. Every time these people start to get bored, they find creative and healthy ways to amuse themselves. In summary, if you want to be a creative person, it's a good idea *not* to watch TV when you get bored.

Part 3
(1) Listen to Student C read the last article.
(2) Then discuss it with your partners, using discussion strategies.

Part 4

Discuss your discussion

(1) Did you use a lot of the strategies you've been practicing?
(2) Which ones did you use?
    Which ones didn't you use? Why not?

B
B
B
B
B
B

Summary Discussion • *131*

Rejoinders

I see.
Oh, yeah?
Really?
That's great!
That's too bad.

Follow-up Questions

(Questions about an answer)

A: **What did you do last night?**
B: **I watched a movie on TV.**
A: *(Rejoinder and Follow-up)* **I see.**
   What movie did you watch?

Format: Triads – Student A, page 1; Student B, page 67

Before the discussion
(1) *Silently* read and answer the questions below for yourself, but *do not write the answers*.
(2) Write two more questions about any topic.

Discussion Directions
(1) Ask *both* of your partners your discussion questions.
(2) After they answer, ask **follow-up questions** and use **rejoinders**.
(3) Take turns. Student A begins with question #1. Student B asks #2, then you ask #3, and you continue.
(4) Answer their questions with details by using *and, but, so, because,* or **two sentences** each time you answer.

Discussion Questions
3 Are you happy now?
6. After getting married, what would cause you to get divorced?
9. Do you enjoy visiting museums?
12. What's your opinion of this group's members?
15. Do your parents treat you and your siblings equally?
18. Do you trust most people?
21. _____?
24. _____?

Note: Follow-up questions frequently use WH-questions.
What movie?   Where did you see it?
Who was in it?   Why did you choose that one?
What did you think of it? How long was it?
How often do you go to the movies?

C C C C C

Rejoinders and Follow-up Questions   **• 133**

Answering with Details

Format: Triads – Student A, page 9; Student B, page 75

Before the discussion
(1) *Silently* read and answer the questions below for yourself, but *do not write the answers*.
(2) Write two more questions about any topic.

Discussion Directions
(1) Ask these questions of *both* of your partners.
(2) After they answer, ask them follow-up questions.
(3) Answer their questions *with details* by using *and, but, so, because,* or **two sentences** each time you answer.

Discussion Questions
Some Personal Questions

3. What brand of car would you like to buy someday?
6. Do all the members of your family usually eat dinner together?
9. How is your health recently?
12. Are you planning to watch TV today?
15. If I were coming to your house for dinner tonight, what would you make for me ?
18. What makes you to feel nervous?
21. _____?
24. _____?

Discussion

Format: Triads – Student A, page 11; Student B, page 77
Topic: Your High School Days

Before the discussion
   (1) *Silently* read the questions below, but *do not write* the
      answers.
   (2) Write two more questions about the topic.

Discussion Directions
   (1) Ask these questions of *both* of your partners.
   (2) After they answer, ask them **follow-up questions**, and use
      rejoinders (e.g. ,"I see," "That's too bad," or "That's great!").
   (3) Also, answer your partners' questions *with details*.

Discussion Questions

Your High School Days

  3. Was your school co-educational (both boys and girls)?

  6. Do you wish you could have gone to a different school?

  9. Did you have any friends of the opposite sex, or were your
     friends the same sex as you?

12. What kinds of things did you enjoy doing in your free time?

15. Were your school rules strict?

18. Were you ever scolded by a teacher?

21. Did your school have special parties, festivals, or other events?

24. Did you have to take any special exams in order to enter your
     high school or to graduate?

27. Did your school have a cafeteria?

30. Which subjects did you hate?

33. What was the most difficult thing for you in those days?

36. _____

39. _____

C
C
C
C
C

Discussion

Paragraph Clarifications, I

Focus: Paragraph-by-paragraph clarifications, with clarification
questions provided
Format: Triads – Student A, page 12; Student B, page 78
Topic: Animals in Movies

Before Part 1 of the discussion
  (1) *Silently* read your part of the article (C) about animals in
      movies in Part 3.
  (2) Write the answers to the *Factual Questions* in Part 4.

Parts 1 & 2
   Listen to Students A & B tell their parts of the story. *After each
paragraph*, ask the appropriate **clarification question** below.

PARAGRAPH 1: Did you say a person was killed in a movie?
PARAGRAPH 2: What did you say "AHS" means?
PARAGRAPH 3: Did you say some people were angry? At whom? Why?
PARAGRAPH 4: Did you say the horses are never hurt? Why (not)?
PARAGRAPH 5: Can you explain again what electronic animals are?
PARAGRAPH 6: I don't understand the word "parachutes."

Part 3
  (1) Read this third part of the story to your partners.
  (2) *Stop after each paragraph* to ask your **comprehension check.**
  (3) Then answer your partners' **clarification questions.**

Animals in Movies (C)

7. We'll continue with the last part of this story. This is paragraph 7.
   When animals are used in movies, the AHS comes to the movie
   set and watches the animals closely, because movie-making can
   be stressful for animals. Lions and tigers become irritable, or
   short-tempered, if they have to wait a long time for their scene.
   Elephants will sway, in other words, move back and forth,
   when they feel stress.
   Do you understand paragraph 7?

This article is continued on the next page.

C
C
C
C
C
C

8. In one movie, they used 50 fish. They needed these fish for 4 days. The AHS made sure that the fish had clean water every day and that the water temperature was correct, in other words, not too hot or too cold.
   Understand the eighth paragraph?

9. The AHS watches every animal in a movie: lions, bears, elephants, dogs, and even bugs (which are insects). For example, the actors in a movie aren't allowed to hurt or kill even cockroaches.
   OK?

Part 4

Factual Questions about the story
Ask your partners the following questions

9. Why do movie animals sometimes feel stress?
   _____
   _____

10. What did the AHS do about the 50 fish that were in a movie?
    _____
    _____

11. What are some animals that are used in movies?
    _____

12. What's a cockroach?
    _____
    _____

Reaction Questions about your partners' opinions and experiences. Ask these questions and ask follow-up questions.

You, Animals, and the Movies

3. In your country, are people sometimes cruel to animals? Explain.
6. How much does it cost to rent a video in your country?
9. Which do you prefer: foreign-made movies or movies made in your own country?
12. (Think of some questions about this topic of movies and animals.)

C
C
C
C
C
C

Paragraph Clarifications, I

Paragraph Clarifications, II

Focus: Paragraph-by-paragraph clarifications, clarification questions *not* provided

Format: **Triads** – Student A, page 14; Student B, page 80

Topic: Sleep

Before Part 1 of the discussion
(1) *Silently* read your part (C) of the article about sleep in Part 3.
(2) Write the answers to the *Factual Questions* about the article.

Parts 1 & 2
(1) Listen to your partners read the rest of the article.
(2) When they ask if you understand, ask your own **clarification questions,** *even if you understand clearly.*

Part 3
(1) Read this third part of the story to your partners.
(2) *Stop after each paragraph* to ask your **comprehension check.**
(3) Answer your partners' **clarification questions.**
(4) Then ask your partners your *Factual Questions.*

Sleep (C)

7. Here is some more advice for good sleep habits. You should get physical exercise every day. If you exercise, you'll get a deeper sleep and you won't need as much sleep.
   Do you understand that paragraph?

8. Next, if you often have trouble sleeping, you should take a hot bath before going to bed, or read a book for pleasure. Also, you should be sure your bedroom is quiet, dark, and cool. If you go to bed and cannot fall asleep within 20 minutes, you should get up and do something else until you're sleepy.
   Got it?

This news story is continued on the next page.

C
C
C
C
C

9. The final piece of advice is about caffeine. You shouldn't drink coffee or tea if you feel sleepy in the middle of the day. Instead of a coffee break, it's better if you take a nap. A 15- to 20-minute nap is very helpful. However, you should not take a nap for more than 20 minutes. If your nap is too long, you'll fall into a deep sleep and you'll feel even more tired when you wake up.
   Understand?

Factual Questions about the article

1. Regarding sleep, what are two good effects that you get from doing physical exercise?

2. If you have trouble sleeping, what are two things you can do?

3. What should you do if you can't fall asleep after 20 minutes?

4. If you get sleepy in the middle of the day, which is better for you, to drink some coffee or to take a nap?

5. Is it good to take a nap for an hour? Why (not)?

6. What happens if your nap is too long?

Part 4

Reaction Questions about your partners' opinions and experiences. Ask these questions and ask follow-up questions.

Sleeping Habits

3. Do you sometimes fall asleep while watching movies or TV, or while reading a book?
6. Are you a deep sleeper or light sleeper? (In other words, do you wake up easily if there is noise?)
9. Do you know anyone who doesn't sleep enough?
12. Do you drink or eat when you feel sleepy during the day?
15. (Think of two more questions about **sleep** and ask your partners.)

C
C
C
C
C
C

Paragraph Clarifications, II

Asking for More Details

> Could you give me an example of _____?
> What do you mean _____?
> Could you explain _____?
> Could you tell me why/who/what _____?
> I'd like to know more about _____.

Format: Triads – Student A, page 16; Student B, page 82

Before the discussion
  (1) *Silently* read the sentences below and fill in the blanks.

Discussion Directions
  (1) Read these sentences to your partners.
  (2) Listen to your partners' sentences. **Ask them for more details**.

Discussion Starters

3. If you were a doctor or psychiatrist, I would ask you for advice about _____

6. When I'm 65 years old, _____

9. _____ is the person I would like to have dinner with some day.

12. There are two main reasons why I'm glad I'm _____ _____: First, _____ _____ And second, _____ _____

15. One thing I hope I never have to do is _____

18. As a child, my favorite toy was _____

C
C
C
C
C

Student C • Unit 10

Discussion

Format: Triads – Student A, page 17; Student B, page 83
Topic: Stress

Before Part 1 of the discussion
(1) **Silently** read your part (C) of the article about stress in Part 3.
(2) Write answers to your *Factual Questions* and then write two more questions.

Parts 1 & 2
(1) Listen to your partners read the first and second parts of the article.
(2) Ask clarification questions when you don't understand.
(3) Answer the *Factual Questions* they ask you.

Part 3
(1) Read this last part of the article (C) to your partners.
(2) Answer any clarification questions they have.
(3) Ask them your *Factual Questions*.

Stress (C)

This is the third part of the article. It is not important that you have a lot of friends. It is important that you have close friends, even if you have only a few. **Understand?** For your health, the most important relationships are with the people whom you see every day, for example, roommates or romantic partners. In a study, the happier roommates were, the healthier they were. When roommates felt stress because they disliked each other, they got more colds and the flu. **Do you understand the word "flu"?** The relationship between romantic partners is deeper than that between roommates, and the statistics showed romantic relations, both good and bad, had a greater effect on health.

This article is continued on page 144.

C
C
C
C
C

142 •

Discussion

The friendliest monkeys were the healthiest

Discussion • 143

Researchers also studied the effect of relationships and stress on heart disease. **OK?** They found that monkeys that were not friendly had more heart disease. They also studied 195 elderly people who had had heart attacks. They found that a year after having their heart attacks elderly people who had close friends and relatives were twice as likely to be alive as elderly people who had no such relationships. **Understand? Do you want me to explain that again?** For example, some of the older people said they had two or more friends; only 27% of them died within the first year. But for those elderly people who said they had no friends, 58% died within the first year after having a heart attack. **Do you understand?**

Factual Questions about the article

1. Which is more important for health: to have a lot of friends, or to have a few close friends? _____

2. What happened to the health of roommates who disliked each other? _____

3. _____

4. _____

Part 4

Reaction Questions about your partners' opinions and experiences. Ask the questions below and ask follow-up questions. Also, answer your partners' questions with details.

Stress in Our Lives

3. If you feel stress, do you get sick (for example, get a cold or flu)?
6. What are some things that cause stress for people in your country?

(Think of two more *Reaction Questions*.)

Discussion

Discussion

Format: **Triads** – Student A, page 21; Student B, page 87
Topic: Your Hometown and Childhood Home

Before the discussion
(1) *Silently* read the discussion questions below, but *do not write* the answers.
(2) Write two more questions about the topic of your hometown and childhood home.

Discussion directions
(1) Ask *both of* your partners your discussion questions.
(2) Try to use these *discussion strategies*.

Discussion Strategies

Ask **follow-up questions** and **solicit more details.**
(e.g., "Could you give me an example?" "What do you mean_____?" or "Could you explain _____?")
Use **rejoinders.**
(e.g., "I see," "That's too bad," or "That's great!")
Answer questions **with details.**
(e.g., answer with *and, but, so, because,* or with *two sentences.)*

Discussion Questions
Your Hometown and Childhood Home

3. Does your hometown have many foreigners?
6. If we visited your hometown together, what would we do?
9. When you're away from your hometown, do you feel homesick?
12. Please describe your bedroom with as many details as possible.
15. If you were going to build a house for yourself, would it be different from your childhood home?
18. Did you have nice neighbors?

21. _____

24. _____

C
C
C
C
U
C

Discussion **• 145**

Student C • Unit 12 ⌒

Interrupting Someone

Excuse me. Could I ask something?
Uhh, sorry for interrupting, but . . .
Excuse me, but I have a question.

Format: Triads – Student A, page 22; Student B, page 88
Topic: Telling Lies

Before Part 1 of the discussion
(1) **Silently** read your part (C) of the article about telling lies in Part 3.
(2) Write answers to your *Factual Questions* about the article .

Part 1
(1) Listen to Student A read the first part of the article.

(2) Interrupt *while* A is reading and ask some **clarification questions** *even if you understand clearly*.

(3) Try to use the **"Interrupting Someone"** expressions.

For example: Uhh, sorry for interrupting, (use A's name) , but I have a question. Could you explain again why a worker will lie to the boss?

Part 2
Listen to Student B, interrupt, and ask clarification questions. Use the **"Interrupting Someone"** expressions.

For example: Excuse me, (use B's name) . I have a question. Why do people tell self-centered lies?

Unit 12 is continued on the next page.

C
C
C
C
C

146 •

Part 3
 (1) Read this third part of the article (C) to your partners.
 (2) ***Don't ask them if they understand***, but answer their
     clarification questions when they interrupt you.
 (3) When you're finished, ask them your *Factual Questions*.

Telling Lies (C)

According to our research, extroverts tell more lies than introverts. Extroverts are people who like to spend a lot of time talking with other people. Introverts are people who prefer quiet time alone reading or with just one or two other people. Introverts tell fewer lies than extroverts. Our reasearch also found that people who worry about what others think of them tell more lies than those who don't.

Here's some other information we learned from the research. People don't think small lies are serious, they don't usually plan in advance to tell lies, and most people don't worry about getting caught telling a lie.

After doing our research, however, we believe that some lies are serious. For example, let's say you want to sell your car, which has a problem with its engine. In order to sell it at a high price, you might tell a lie by saying that your car has no problems. In this case, you influenced someone to do something by telling a lie. That is a serious lie.

Finally, our research suggests that being honest all the time *isn't* a good idea. When we insist on telling the truth, we can hurt other people's feelings. If we were always completely honest, we might not have many friends.

C
C
C
C
C

Unit 12 is continued on the next page.

Factual Questions about the article

1. What do you call people who talk a lot with other people?

   _____

2. Who tells more lies, introverts or extroverts?

   _____

3. Do people usually plan to tell lies in advance?

   _____

4. Was the example about selling a car with a bad engine an example of a little lie or a serious lie?

   _____

5. Why are lies sometimes a good idea?

   _____

Part 4

Reaction Questions about your partners' opinions and experiences. Ask these questions and follow-up questions.

To Lie or Not to Lie

3. Let's say you're renting an apartment. One day, you accidentally make a hole in the wall. The landlord says it will cost $30 to fix. Would you tell the landlord the truth, or would you say that the hole was already there?

6. If you wanted to sell something (for example, a car, a CD player, or a bike) but you knew there was a small problem with it, would you tell a person who was interested in buying it?

9. What polite lie have you told recently?

12. Do you worry about people lying to you? If so, in what kind of situation?

Interrupting Someone

Words That Describe

Expressions

It is a person/animal/place/thing that ____.
It is an event/condition/situation that ____.
It is a type/kind/sort of ____.
You can find it at/in ____.

Format: Triads – Student A, page 25; Student B, page 91

Before starting
(1) *Silently* look the words in the list below.
(2) *Don't show or tell your words to your partners.*

Directions
(1) Take turns. Using the expressions above, describe your
    words to your partners.
(2) Don't say the word.
(3) They will try to guess the word.
(4) If they cannot guess the word, they can ask a question.

museum	problem	Olympics	mosquito
politics	extrovert	barefoot	nap
fib	cockroach	flu	jogging
	psychiatrist		

Dropping a butter knife during a meal means a male visitor is forthcoming

Discussion

Format: Triads – Student A, page 27; Student B, page 93
Topic: Superstitions

Before Part 1 of the discussion
(1) *Silently* read your part of the article (C) in Part 3 below.
(2) Write answers to the *Factual Questions* and write two
    more questions.

Parts 1 & 2
(1) Listen to your partners read the first and second parts of
    the article.
(2) *Interrupt and ask clarification questions* when you don'tt
    understand.
(3) Answer your partners' *Factual Questions*.

Part 3
(1) Read this last part of the article to your partners.
(2) Then ask your *Factual Questions*.

Superstitions (C)

According to experts who study Russian culture, there is a
reason why Russians have become more serious about
traditional superstitions. After the communist system
ended some years ago, there was instability in Russia;
people began looking for something that they could believe
in. For this reason, Russians became more interested in
traditional religions and superstitions. **Is that clear?**

Although belief in superstitions seems strongest among old
people and people in the countryside, experts say that we
can find it everywhere in Russian society. For example,
shaking hands in a doorway is considered bad luck by even
some educated Russians. There's an interesting example of
this concerning a Russian cosmonaut. The cosmonaut was

This article is continued on the next page.

C
C
C
C
C

Discussion

• *151*

on the Russian space station when it connected with the American space shuttle. After the space station and space shuttle joined, a door between the two was opened and the American astronaut reached out (or extended) his hand through the doorway to greet the Russians with a handshake. As we know, Russians generally believe shaking hands through a doorway is bad luck, so, at first, the cosmonaut would not do it. However, after a few moments' hesitation, he decided to shake hands anyway even though it might be risky. **Understand?**

Factual Questions about the article

1. What caused Russians to begin looking for something that they could believe in?

_____

2. Who seems to believe in superstitions the most?

_____

3. _____

4. _____

Reaction Questions about your partners' opinions and experiences

(1) Ask these questions and then follow-up questions.
(2) Answer your partners' questions with details.

It's Your Lucky Day

3. Do you know anyone who is superstitious?
6. Have you had any experiences with good or bad luck because of something you did?

(Think of two more *Reaction Questions* about superstitions.)

⁓ *Unit 15* • *Student C*
Telling What You've Heard

┌─── **Phrases for Telling** ───┐

A told me about . . . .
B said (that) . . . .
C told me (that) . . . .
B explained (that) . . . .
According to A, ...

Format: **Triads** – Student A, page 29; Student B, page 95
Topics: Part 1. Short People Live Longer
        Part 2. Gossiping
        Part 3. Why the French Have Fewer Heart Attacks

Before the discussion
(1) *Silently* read your article in Part 3.
(2) Write the answers to the *Factual Questions* about the article.

Part 1
(1) Leave your group and sit in a different part of the room. *Do not listen* to Student A's article.
(2) After Student A tells Student B about the article, come back to the group. Student B will explain the article to you.
(3) Answer Student A's *Factual Questions* about the article.

Part 2
(1) Listen to Student B tell you about the article, "Gossiping." ***Don't take notes.***
(2) Tell Student A about the article.
(3) Student A will answer Student B's *Factual Questions* about the article. ***Don't answer or help.***

Part 3
(1) Tell Student A about your article, "Why the French Have Fewer Heart Attacks."
(2) Do *not* tell Student B.
(3) Student A will tell B what they heard about the article.
(4) Then you ask Student B your *Factual Questions* below.

Unit 15 is continued on the next page.

C
C
C
C
C
C

Telling What You Have Heard   • *153*

Why the French Have Fewer Heart Attacks

Many people are surprised to learn that French people have fewer heart attacks than people in many other countries. When we think of French food, we often imagine sauces that have a lot of fat in them. Some scientists think the reason why the French have fewer heart attacks is that they drink wine with their meals. However, there may be another reason why they have fewer heart attacks.

Researchers studied the diets of 40 countries. They found that the French eat a lot of vegetables, compared to people in other countries. For example, people in Finland drink a lot of milk and eat a lot of dairy products, like eggs and cheese. But Finns don't eat as many vegetables. Researchers found that the Finns had more heart attacks than the French; in fact, the Finns had five times as many heart attacks as the French.

So the researchers say that eating a lot of vegetables is very good for our health. And they warn that, if we drink wine, we shouldn't drink too much. They say that eating extra carrots isn't dangerous, but drinking an extra glass of wine might be.

Unit 15 is continued on the next page.

C
C
C
C
C

Telling What You've Heard

Factual Questions about the article, "Why the French Have Fewer Heart Attacks"

1. Is this true or false? French people have more heart attacks than other Europeans. _____

2. What the French drink with meals?

   _____

3. What do the French eat a lot of?

   _____

4. Why do people in Finland have a lot of heart attacks?

   _____

5. Finns had how many times more heart attacks than the French? _____

6. Which is safer, drinking an extra glass of wine or eating extra carrots? _____

Part 4

Reaction Questions about your partners opinions and experiences. Discussion about the article, "Why the French Have Fewer Heart Attacks"

Your Feelings about Eating a Healthy Diet

11. Do you feel that you have a healthy diet?
12. How many times a day do you eat vegetables?
13. What's your favorite food?
14. What types of food do you dislike?
15. Have you ever eaten French food? Chinese? Italian? Thai? Turkish? Mexican?

C
C
C
C
C

Volunteering an Answer

┌ Phrases for Volunteering ┐

I think (that) . . .

In my opinion, . . .

I'd like to say (that) . . .

May I say (that) . . .?

Can I answer that?

Can I respond to that?

Format: Small Groups – A, p. 32; B, p. 98; D. p. 157; E. p.158

Directions for Asking

(1) Ask your questions below in any order.

(2) ***Do not ask anyone directly*** (i.e., don't look at anyone or say anyone's name).

[Note: "i.e." is an academic abbreviation meaning "that is" or "in other words."]

(3) Your partners will volunteer to answer.

Directions for Volunteering

(1) ***Volunteer to answer*** your partners' questions ***with details*** (answer with **and, but, so, because,** or **two sentences**).

(2) Try to answer first sometimes, and sometimes wait for your partners to volunteer.

(3) Ask follow-up questions, too.

Questions for volunteers to answer

- Do you have a lucky or favorite number?
- What's the most beautiful place in your country?
- Did you have a hobby as a child?
- Would you marry someone who wanted to be a farmer?
- If you bought a car today, what color would you choose?
- (You think of some questions.)

C
C
C
C
C
C

Volunteering an Answer

┌─ Phrases for Volunteering ─┐

I think (that) . . .
In my opinion, . . .
I'd like to say (that) . . .
May I say (that) . . .?
Can I answer that?
Can I respond to that?

Format: Small Groups – A, p. 32; B, p. 98; C, p. 156; E, p. 158

Directions for Asking

(1) Ask your questions below in any order.
(2) ***Do not ask anyone directly*** (i.e., don't look at anyone or say anyone's name).

[Note: "i.e." is an academic abbreviation meaning "that is" or "in other words."]

(3) Your partners will volunteer to answer.

Directions for Volunteering

(1) ***Volunteer to answer*** your partners' questions ***with details*** (answer with **and, but, so, because,** or **two sentences**).
(2) Try to answer first sometimes, and sometimes wait for your partners to volunteer.
(3) Ask follow-up questions, too.

Questions for volunteers to answer

- Which do you prefer: team sports like basketball or individual sports like tennis?
- What color is the top blanket on your bed?
- What company would you like to work for?
- If you have trouble falling asleep, what do you do?
- What's the most expensive thing you own?
- (You think of some questions.)

D
D
D
D
D

Volunteering an Answer

Phrases for Volunteering

> I think (that) . . .
> In my opinion, . . .
> I'd like to say (that) . . .
> May I say (that) . . . ?
> Can I answer that?
> Can I respond to that?

Format: Small Groups – A, p. 32; B, p. 98; C, p. 156; D, p. 157

Directions for Asking

(1) Ask your questions below in any order.

(2) ***Do not ask anyone directly*** (i.e., don't look at anyone or say anyone's name).

[Note: "i.e." is an academic abbreviation meaning "that is" or "in other words."]

(3) Your partners will volunteer to answer.

Directions for Volunteering

(1) ***Volunteer to answer*** your partners' questions ***with details*** (answer with **and, but, so, because,** or **two sentences**).

(2) Try to answer first sometimes, and sometimes wait for your partners to volunteer.

(3) Ask follow-up questions, too.

Questions for volunteers to answer

- What actor or actress would you like to meet?
- Would you marry a foreigner?
- Are you a "morning person" or a "night person"?
- What did you buy the last time you went shopping?
- What animal would you like to be?
- (You think of some questions.)

E
E
E
E
E

Discussion

Format: Triads – Student A, page 33; Student B, page 99
Topic: Divorce

Part 1

Pre-discussion
  (1) Before starting this discussion of divorce in Europe, ask
      your partners these questions.
  (2) Answer their questions.

  3. Which of these countries do you think has the highest divorce
     rate? (a) Britain (b) Sweden (c) Spain (d) Greece
  6. In general, what do you think is the most common reason for
     divorce?
     a) The couple doesn't have similar interests.
     b) Violence, i.e., the husband or wife hits or beats the other
        one.
     c) Poor communication, in other words, the spouses don't talk
        to each other much or they often have disagreements.
     d) The husband or wife has a secret lover.

Part 2

Discussion Directions
  (1) Listen to Student A read the first part of the article.
  (2) Listen to Student B read the second part of the article.
  (3) Read your third part of the article to your partners.

DIVORCE (C)

It's interesting to see why the divorce rate is lower in some
European countries than in others. In Italy, there are
few divorces, probably because Italians believe marriages
should continue forever. Furthermore, in general, Italian

This news story continues on the next page.

C
C
C
C
C

Discussion   **• 159**

women cannot make as much money as men, so they need men's financial support. Finally, in Italy having a lover outside of marriage is widely acceptable. In other words, most Italians would not want a divorce if they found out that their spouse had a secret lover.

Another country with a low divorce rate is Spain. Actually, divorce was illegal in Spain until 1981. Also, like Italian women, Spanish women need men's financial support. But the most important reason why the divorce rate is low in Spain is that the extended family is very important there. In an extended family, children, parents, grandparents and even great-grandparents live together. Spanish men feel it is their responsibility to stay with their families and take care of their children.

Finally, what are the reasons people get divorced? The most common reason is violence, when one of the spouses hits or beats the other one. Some other reasons are (1) the couple is unable to communicate with each other, (2) a spouse has a secret lover, (3) a spouse has a problem with alcohol or drugs, and (4) the couple has no common interest.

Part 3

Factual Questions about the news story

Read the questions in Part 1 to your partners again and try to answer their questions.

Part 4

Reaction Questions about your partners' opinions

Your Feelings about Marriage and Divorce

3. What do you think is a good age to get married?
6. When you were a child, did you live with an extended family? Do you think it was good that your grandparents did or didn't live with you?
9. Is it common for women in your country to have children outside of marriage?

Discussion   • *161*

C
C
C
C
C
C

Clarifying by Summarizing, II

Focus: Summarizing (clarifications are not provided)
Format: Triads – Student A, page 40; Student B, page 105
Topic: Catching Colds

Before Part 1 of the discussion

(1) *Silently* read this last part of the article (C) in Part 3.
(2) Write answers to the *Factual Questions* in Part 4.

Parts 1 & 2

(1) Listen to your partners read the first two parts of the article.
(2) Ask **summary clarification questions** when asked if you understand, *even if you do understand clearly*.
(3) Use the following expressions.

┌─ **Summary Clarification Questions** ─┐

Did you say _____?   **You mean _____?**

You said _____, right? In other words, _____, right?

I think you said _____, right?

I'm not sure I understand. Did you say _____?

Part 3

(1) Read this last part of the article to your partners.
(2) Answer their **summary clarification questions**.

Catching Colds (C)

How do we know when we're catching a cold? Usually, a cold starts in our throat; we start to feel a sore throat. Then the cold moves to our nose, and we start to have a runny nose. Our bodies will start to fight the cold and, after about a week, our bodies will win the fight and we will feel healthy again. **Have you got this first paragraph?**

This news story is continued on the next page.

C
C
C
C
C

If our cold continues for more than two weeks, it probably means we don't really have a cold at all. Instead, we may have something more serious. In that case, we should go to a doctor. **Understand?**

The average adult gets two or three colds every year. On the other hand, children and teenagers get five to ten colds a year. This is because adults have developed a defense system against the types of colds they had when they were younger. But children need to catch a cold first in order to build a defense. Also, children catch more colds because they don't wash their hands often and because often they put their hands in their mouths after touching something dirty. **Got it?**

Part 4

Factual Questions about the article
Ask these questions and answer your partners'.

3. Where do we first feel a cold in our bodies?

6. If you have a cold for more than two weeks, what should you do? Why?

9. Who gets more colds every year, adults or children? Why?

Reaction Questions about your partners' opinions and experiences. Ask these questions and ask follow-up questions.

You and the Common Cold

3. When you were younger, did you ever miss several days of school because you were sick?
6. What health problem have you had recently?
9. Do you think your hometown is a healthy place to live?

C
C
C
C
U
C

Telling Other People's Opinions and Experiences

Format: Small Groups – A, page 42; B, page 107; D, page 166

Part 1

(1) Discuss the *topics* below with your partners.

(2) Try to give details and ask questions to get more details.

(3) Listen closely to what your partners say, because in Part 2 you will tell new groups what they said.

Discussion topics

3. Tell us what you were doing last year at this time.

7. Tell us about the job you would like to have in the future.

Expressions for Telling Others' Opinions and Experiences

I have no opinion about that,
    but I know someone who . . .
I haven't, but _____ **has.**
           (friend's name)

I've never done that, but my friend . . .
I'm not sure, but someone told me . . .
I don't know, but I do know someone who . . .

Part 2

(1) Get into new groups.

(2) Ask your new partners the questions below. Answer their questions by telling what you learned in your first group in Part 1. Use the expressions for "Telling Others' Opinions and Experiences."

(3) ***Do not tell your own opinions or experiences***.

(4) Ask questions to get more details.

Unit 20 continues on the next page.

C
C
C
C
C

Student C • Unit 20, continued

Discussion questions
3. What were you doing last year at this time?
7. What job would you like to have in the future?

Part 3
(1) Discuss the *topics* below with your partners.
(2) Try to give details and ask questions to get more details.
(3) Listen closely to what your partners say, because in Part 4
  you will form a new group and tell what they said.

More discussion topics
3. Tell us about a movie you've seen recently.
7. Tell us the name of a famous person you would like to be.

Part 4

Directions
(1) Get into new groups again.
(2) Ask your new partners the questions below. Answer
  their questions by telling what you learned in your second
  group in Part 3. Use the expressions for "Telling Others'
  Opinions and Experiences."
(3) ***Do not give your own opinions or experiences***.
(4) Ask questions to get more details.

More discussion questions
3. Have you seen any movies recently?
7. What famous person would you like to be?

C
C
C
C
C

Telling Other People's Opinions and Experiences • *165*

Student D • Unit 20 ⌒

Telling Other People's Opinions and Experiences

Format: Small Groups – A, page 42; B, page 107; C, page 164

Part 1
   (1) Discuss the *topics* below with your partners.
   (2) Try to give details and ask questions to get more details.
   (3) Listen closely to what your partners say, because in Part 2
       you will tell new groups what they said.

Discussion topics
   4. Tell us about one of your recent problems.
   8. Tell us about a famous person you've met.

Expressions for Re-telling Others' Opinions and Experiences

I have no opinion about that,
      but I know someone who . . .
I haven't, but _____ has.
          (friend's name)
I've never done that, but my friend . . .
I'm not sure, but someone told me . . .
I don't know, but I do know someone who . . .

Part 2
   (1) Get into new groups.
   (2) Ask your new partners the questions below. Answer
       their questions by telling what you learned in your first
       group in Part 1. Use the expressions for "Telling Others'
       Opinions and Experiences."
   (3) ***Do not tell your own opinions or experiences***.
   (4) Ask questions to get more details.

Unit 20 continues on the next page.

Discussion questions

4. What problem have you had recently?
8. What famous person have you met?

Part 3

(1) Discuss the *topics* below with your partners.
(2) Try to give details and ask questions to get more details.
(3) Listen closely to what your partners say, because in Part 4 you will form a new group and tell what they said.

More discussion topics

4. Tell us about a time when you were punished by your teacher or parents.
8. Tell us about an insect or animal that you're afraid of or that disgusts you.

Part 4

Directions

(1) Get into new groups again.
(2) Ask your new partners the questions below. Answer their questions by telling what you learned in your second group in Part 3. Use the expressions for "Telling Others' Opinions and Experiences."
(3) **Do not give your own opinions or experiences**.
(4) Ask questions to get more details.

More discussion questions

4. Were you ever punished by your teacher or parents?
8. Are you afraid of any animals or insects?

D
D
D
D
D

Discussion

Format: **Triads** – Student A, page 44; Student B, page 109
Topic: Driving

Before Part 1 of the discussion
(1) *Silently* read your article about driving in Part 3.
(2) Write answers to your *Factual Questions* and write two more questions.
(3) Write two more *Reaction Questions* in Part 4.

Parts 1 & 2
(1) Listen to your partners read the first and second articles.
(2) Interrupt to ask them clarification questions when you don't understand.
(3) Answer their *Factual Questions*.

Part 3
(1) Read this last article to your partners.
(2) Then ask your *Factual Questions*.

Driving a Stolen Car

Mike Morris wanted to go to the grocery store, but he couldn't use his car because his mother's blue van was parked behind his in the driveway. So he borrowed his mother's van and drove to a shopping center. After buying some groceries and putting them in the van, he decided to shop in a couple of other stores at the shopping center. When he returned to the blue van, he noticed that his bags of groceries were gone, so he thought someone had broken into the van and stolen them. As he was

This story continues on the next page.

driving back home, he suddenly heard some police sirens and noticed flashing lights behind him. He stopped his van, got out, and saw five policemen with their guns pointed at him. Then he realized his mistake; he had taken the wrong blue van. Surprisingly, the key to his mother's van also worked in the other van, too! After returning to the shopping center with Mike and seeing his mother's van, the police believed his story and let him go.

Factual Questions about your article

Ask your partners these questions.

1. Why didn't Mike drive his car to the shopping center?

   _____

2. What did he do after he bought some groceries?

   _____

3. _____

4. _____

Part 4

Reaction Questions about your partners' opinions and experiences

Ask these reaction questions and some follow-up questions. Write two more questions to ask. Answer your partners' questions with details.

Stolen Cars

9. In your country, is it necessary to lock your car doors whenever you leave your car in a parking lot?

10. Have you ever been in a car that was stopped by the police?

11. _____

12. _____

C
C
C
C
C
C

Discussion

Helping the Discussion Leader Explain, I

Format: Triads – Student A, page 47; Student B, page 112

─── Expressions ───

Could you help me explain that?
Do you know what I mean?

─── Example ───

A: When I got up this morning, I felt irritable.
B: What do you mean by "irritable"?
A (to Student C): Could you help me explain that?
C (to Student B): Sure. He means he was in a
  bad mood. He was cross, grumpy, and mad at the
  world when he got up this morning.

Part 1
(1) Student A will read some sentences to Student B.
(2) Student B will ask Student A clarification questions.
(3) Student A will ask you to help clarify for Student B. Help
    Student A explain. Try to have a brief discussion about the
    topic of each sentence.

Unit 22 continues on the next page.

C
C
C
C
C
C

Part 2
   (1) Student B will read some sentences to you.
   (2) You ask Student B the five clarification questions below.
   (3) Student B will ask Student A to help clarify the sentences
        for you.

    1. <u>(Student B)</u>, I'm afraid I don't know what "athlete" means.

    2. Can you give me an example of a pet?

    3. I'm not sure I understand the word "stress." Can you give
       me some examples of what happens to a person who's
       feeling stress?

    4. I'm not sure I understand the question.

    5. What do you mean by the word "homesick"?

Part 3
   (1) Read the following sentences to Student A.
   (2) Student A will ask you to clarify, but **you don't clarify.**
   (3) Ask Student B to help you explain the sentences. Try to
        have a brief discussion about the topic of each of these
        sentences.

    1. <u>(Student A)</u>, is there much crime in your hometown?
       After Student C's clarification question:
       <u>(Student B)</u>, could you help me explain?

    2. When I was a child and did something naughty, my
       parents spanked me.

    3. What were some things you worried about when you were
       a pre-teen?

    4. Did you belong to any clubs when you were in high school?

    5. When I was younger, I often got poor grades because I had
       bad study habits.

C
C
C
C
C
C

Helping the Discussion
Leader Explain, II

Format: Triads – Student A, page 49; Student B, page 114
Topic: Part 1. Fathers Who Live Longer
         Part 2. Smoking and Aging
         Part 3. Tasting Foods

Before Part 1 of the discussion
(1) *Silently* read your article about tasting food in Part 3.
(2) Write answers to your *Factual Questions* and write two
    more questions.
(3) Write two more *Reaction Questions* in Part 4.

Parts 1 & 2
(1) Listen to your partners read their articles.
(2) For practice, ask **clarification questions**, *even if you*
    understand clearly.

Part 3
(1) Read this article to your partners.
(2) Don't answer your partners' clarification questions.
(3) Ask a partner to help you explain.
(4) Try to use the **"Help the Leader" Expressions.**
(5) Ask your *Factual Questions.*

"Help the Leader"
Expressions

Could you help me explain that?
Do you know what I mean?

C
C
C
C
C
C

Unit 23 continues on the next page.

Tasting Food

Scientists have been studying the reasons why some people don't like the taste of certain vegetables. They found that people inherit some genes from their parents that cause them to like or dislike certain tastes. **Did you understand?**

In their research about tastes, scientists found that there are three types of people in the world. First, there are "nontasters," who are not very sensitive to sweet-tasting foods or bitter-tasting foods. The people of the second type are just called "tasters," and those of the third are "supertasters," who are very sensitive to sweet and bitter flavors. Children of the third type, who are supertasters, will probably not like vegetables such as broccoli and brussel sprouts because of their bitter taste. This is unfortunate, because supertasters might avoid eating foods that are important for their health. **OK?**

The scientists said that thousands of years ago, on the other hand, supertasters actually had an advantage over other types of people. At that time, supertasters could avoid eating bitter-tasting poisonous plants which other types of people would eat. **Got it?**

From this research about tastes, we learn some interesting things about supertasters. For one thing, supertasters have more taste buds on their tongues. And, to supertasters, bitter foods taste *very* bitter, and sweet foods taste *very* sweet. Supertasters might also not like spicy food made with chili pepper, because it would be too hot for them. Furthermore, female supertasters probably won't be very fat, but they do seem to enjoy cooking more than other types of people. **Understand?**

C
C
C
C
C
C

Factual Questions about the article

Ask these questions about the article.

1. _____

2. What are the three types of people in the world?

_____

3. Is this statement true or false? Thousands of years ago, supertasters probably ate many poisonous plants.

_____

4. _____

Parts 2 & 3

(1) Listen to your partners read their articles.
(2) For practice, ask **clarification questions**, *even if you understand clearly*.

Part 4

Reaction Questions about your partners' opinions and experiences

1. About the article on tasting food, do you think you're a supertaster?
2. In general, do you prefer the food from your own country or from other countries?

3. _____

4. _____

C
C
C
C
C
C

Helping the Discussion Leader Explain, II   **• 175**

Discussion

Format: Triads – Student A, page 52; Student B, page 117
Topic: Gambling

Before Part 1 of the discussion
   (1) *Silently* read your part of the article about gambling in Part 3.
   (2) Write answers to your *Factual Questions* and write two
       more questions.

Parts 1 & 2
   (1) Listen to your partners read the first two parts of the article.
   (2) Interrupt to ask them clarification questions when you don't
       understand.
   (3) Answer their *Factual Questions*.

Part 3
   (1) Read this last part of the article to your partners.
   (2) Then ask them your *Factual Questions*.

Gambling (C)

Here is a story about a woman who became a compulsive
gambler. Her name is Rose. She was a wife and mother who
lived in a comfortable suburb of New York. Rose had never
gambled in her life because it was illegal — until New York
State started a lottery. Then she bought some lottery tickets.

After a few weeks, Rose won some money. She felt confident that
she would soon become a millionaire. So she started to play other
lottery games, too, and started spending $100 and then $300 a week.
Soon she had spent all the money in her family's bank account and
started using her credit cards to borrow more money for gambling.

This article continues on the next page.

Her family didn't know about her gambling problems. After her husband got sick and died, she started gambling even more. Soon she owed more than $100,000. In the end, she was able to stop gambling only after joining an organization that helps compulsive gamblers control their habit.

Factual Questions about your article

Ask your partners these questions.

1. _____

2. What was the first thing Rose gambled on?

   _____

3. Why didn't she quit gambling after she lost money?

   _____

4. _____

Part 4

Reaction Questions about your partners' opinions and experiences. Ask the questions below and some follow-up questions. Answer your partners' questions with details.

Lady Luck and You

3. Do you know anyone who is compulsive (for example, a compulsive shopper, eater, worker, or computer-game player)?

6. Have you ever borrowed money for anything?

(Think of two more *Reaction Questions* about gambling.)

C
C
C
C
C

Expressing Opinions, II

Format: **Small Groups** – A, page 58; B, page 123; D, page 182
Topics: Part 1. The Rights of Mothers and Fathers
Part 2. Death Caused by Cigarettes
Part 3. Circus Animals
Part 4. 63-year-old Woman Has a Baby

Agreeing

That's a good point.
I totally agree with _____.
That's right.

Disagreeing

I'm afraid I disagree.
That's a good point, but . . .
Actually, I think . . .

Before Part 1 of the discussion
Silently read this article about circus animals in Part 3.

Parts 1 & 2
(1) Listen to Students A & B read the first and second articles.
(2) Answer and discuss their questions.

Part 3
(1) Read your article to your partners.
(2) Then ask the *Factual* and *Reaction Questions*.

Unit 26 is continued on the next page.

C
C
C
C
C

Circus Animals

The death of two elephants at a circus in Los Angeles has caused an argument between animal rights groups and circus groups. For over 100 years, elephant performances have attracted people to circuses. But animal rights groups say circuses often don't take care of the elephants or other wild animals. They found that some animal trainers beat the animals or use electric shocks in order to teach them to do tricks. They said circus animals spend much of their time tied up or in traveling trailers, where there is neither heat nor air conditioning. Also, according to animal rights groups, animals aren't given water or food before they perform, because the circus doesn't want them to create a mess in the circus rings by urinating and defecating during a show.

Circus owners disagree. They say that their elephants are part of their family. Owners have said that without elephants, most of the circuses would have to close. In fact, one circus tried to stop using elephants but attendance dropped, and many people said that they wanted to see more animals. According to one circus worker, small circuses visit many towns that do not have zoos. So, often a circus is the only place where small-town children can see wild animals.

Factual Questions about the article
  Ask these questions about the article.

1. What do animal rights groups say about circus animals?
2. What do circus owners say about their animals?

Reaction Questions about your partners' opinions. Ask these questions about the article. Agree or disagree with your partners. Express your own opinions as well.

Animal Rights and Captive Animals

1. What do you think should be done about circus animals?
2. What is you opinion of zoos? Should they be illegal?

Part 4

(1) Listen to Student D read the last article.
(2) Answer and discuss their questions.

C
C
C
C
C

Expressing Opinions, II

Format: Small Groups – A, page 58; B, page 123; C, page 179
Topics: Part 1.   The Rights of Mothers and Fathers
　　　　Part 2.   Death Caused by Cigarettes
　　　　Part 3.   Circus Animals
　　　　Part 4.   63-year-old Woman Has a Baby

Agreeing

That's a good point.
I totally agree with _____.
That's right.

Disagreeing

I'm afraid I disagree.
That's a good point, but . . .
Actually, I think . . .

Before Part 1 of the discussion
　　Silently read this article about the 63-year-old woman having a baby in Part 4.

Parts 1, 2, & 3
　　(1)   Listen to Students A, B, & C read their articles.
　　(2)   Answer and discuss their questions.

Part 4
　　(1)   Read your article to your partners.
　　(2)   Then ask the *Factual* and *Reaction Questions*.

Unit 26 is continued on the next page.

63-year-old Woman Has a Baby

Recently, a woman who was 63 years old had a baby. Even though she was past the age when a woman can get pregnant naturally, she was able to do it through a laboratory. Some people think that a woman at this age shouldn't have a baby; others think she has a right to.

The woman said she wanted to have a baby because she had never had any children, and she wanted to experience childbirth. Besides, she wanted someone to continue her family's name. People who agree with her decision say that she will be a better mother than many younger mothers because she is mature and has a lot of life experiences. They also say she has more time to spend with her child than many younger mothers, who are busy with their careers and other activities; moreover, she has more money to spend on her child than many young mothers do. Finally, they say few people become upset when men in their 60s became fathers, so it's only fair that women should also be able to.

People who oppose her decision to have a baby say it's unnatural for women at this age to have babies. They say a woman in her 60s shouldn't need to get pregnant in order to feel valuable. These people also say that it's not fair to the child. When the child is 15, her mother will be 78. This teenage child will have the responsibility that many people in their 40s and 50s have of taking care of older relatives. It will be like a teenager taking care of her grandparents.

D
D
D
D
D

Factual Questions about the article

Ask these questions about the article.

1. Why did this woman decide to have a baby?
2. Why do some people disagree with her decision?

Reaction Questions about your partners' opinions. Ask these questions about the article. Agree or disagree with your partners. Express your own opinions as well.

Too Old for Motherhood?

1. Do you think that it ws a good idea for this woman to have a baby?
2. Should there be a law against older women having babies?

Referring to a Source

Format: **Triads** – Student A, page 61; Student B, page 126
Topic: Bullying

┌─ Referring to a Source ─┐

I read that _____.
I heard that _____.
According to an article I read, _____.
According to the newspaper, _____.

Before Part 1 of the discussion
(1) *Silently* read the information from the article about bullying.
(2) **Do not read this article to your partners.**

Bullying (C)

This article about bullying explains what can be done to help children who are victims of bullying, and what the victims themselves can do to stop the bullies.

There are several things parents can do if their child is a victim of bullying. One thing is to practice with the child what to say or do when the bully tries to hurt them. In other words, the parents and child can role play; the kid plays the part of the bully, and the parent plays the part of the victim. Also, parents can help children make friends by encouraging them to invite classmates to their home or by encouraging the children to join clubs. Parents can also help siblings to get along. Kids who have close relationships with friends and siblings will have a feeling of support when confronted by a bully.

Some cities that have bullying problems have 24-hour hot lines that victims can call if they need help and advice.

This article is continued on the next page.

C
C
C
C
C

There are also some things victims can do to discourage bullies. First, the victim shouldn't react by crying. A bully is trying to get a reaction, so if the victim can remain calm, then the bully won't be rewarded. Second, the victim can respond but not fight back. They can say to the bully, "Don't do that. I'll report you." The victim can also try to explain to the bully how they feel; however, it's a good idea to do this when the bully is alone instead of when they're with their friends. Finally, it's a good idea for the victim to have friends around when the bully is near. **Source:** *The Observer*

Parts 1 & 2

Answer your partners' questions by giving your opinion. You don't have to refer to a source.

Part 3

(1) Don't read this article to your partners.
(2) Instead, ask the following questions.
(3) After your partners answer, tell them what you have learned from the article. Don't read it to them.
(4) Try to use the expressions for **"Referring to a Source."**

Questions for your partners

1. What do you think parents can do to help a child who is the victim of a bully?
2. What do you think kids should do if they're victims of bullying?

Part 4

Discussion about your partners' opinions and experiences with bullying. Ask your partners these questions, and answer their questions.

3. When you were younger, did you ever have a fight with anyone?
6. In school, did you ever help another student who was a victim of bullying?

Referring to a Source

Summary Discussion

Format: Triads – Student A, page 64; Student B, page 129
Topics: Part 1. Best Friends
Part 2. The Effects of Watching TV
Part 3. Spanking

Before Part 1
(1) Review the Discussion Strategies with your partner(s).
(2) First, fill in the blanks in the Summary box below by asking each other for examples.
(3) Then go back to the unit where the strategy is introduced to review other phrases and expressions.
(4) Then *silently* read your article in Part 1.

Discussion Strategies Summary

Rejoinders (Unit 1)	_____
Follow-up Questions (Unit 1)	_____
Clarification Expressions (Unit 2)	*Did you say that . . . ?*
Comprehension Checks (Unit 3)	_____
Answering with Details (Unit 5)	_____
Interrupting (Unit 12)	*Could I ask something?*
Words That Describe (Unit 13)	_____
Re-telling Something (Unit 15)	_____
Volunteering an Answer (Unit 16)	*May / Can I answer that?*
Summary Clarification Questions (Unit 19)	_____
Re-telling Others' Opinions (Unit 20)	_____
Helping the Leader (Unit 22)	*Could you help me explain that?*
Expressing Opinions (Unit 25)	_____
Referring to a Source (Unit 27)	_____

C
C
C
C
C

Parts 1 & 2
  (1) Listen to your partners read their articles.
  (2) Then discuss their articles with them, using discussion
      strategies.

Part 3
  (1) Read this article to your partners.
  (2) Then discuss it, using the strategies above.

Spanking

This article talks about spanking children. Researchers
have discovered that problems are caused when parents
spank their children. They found that hitting children
actually makes them behave even worse than before.
In other words, spanking children increases aggressive
behavior.

Parents often think that by using corporal punish-
ment, they will make their children behave better. This
may be true at first, but a month or even a year later,
these kids show antisocial behavior. Some examples of
antisocial behavior are lying, cheating, bullying,
breaking things on purpose, disobeying teachers, and
not apologizing.

Researchers compared the behavior of children who
had and hadn't been spanked. Over a two-year period,
they interviewed 800 mothers of children between the
ages of six and nine. The week before the interview,

This article continues on the next page.

C
C
C
C
C

44% of the mothers had spanked their children an average of twice during that week. The results showed that the more children were spanked, the more they behaved in an antisocial manner. Many people think that if parents hit their children "because they love them," there will be no harmful effect. However, research shows that this is not true.

Part 4

Discuss your discussion

(1) Did you use a lot of the strategies you've been practicing?
(2) Which ones did you use?
   Which ones didn't you use? Why not?

C
C
C
C
C

A Teacher-led Discussion

Format: Whole-class or **large-group**
Topic: Working Mothers

For Teachers Only
Possible formats:
(1) The teacher models as a leader of a whole-class discussion.
(2) In a class with strong discussion skills, one or two students serve as a leaders of a whole-class discussion.
(3) With a large and strong class divided, several students serve as leaders of large-group discussions.

Procedure
(1) The *leader(s)* silently reads the article about working mothers and writes several *Factual and Reaction Questions*.
(2) The *leader* reads the article and leads a discussion by asking the questions. The *members* should be encouraged to interrupt and use discussion strategies such as asking clarification questions, volunteering to answer, answering with details, helping the leader, and so on.

Working Mothers

Forty or fifty years ago, it was quite common for mothers to stay home to take care of their children. But nowadays, many mothers have jobs outside the home. In fact, it isn't unusual for some mothers to return to their jobs within a few weeks of having a baby. Some people with traditional values, however, feel it is important for mothers to stay home with the children, especially with babies. People on opposite sides of this issue may

This article is continued on the next page.

A Model Teacher-led Discussion

never agree on which way is better, but recently there has been some surprising research on the effects that working mothers have on their children.

In order to learn whether it's important for mothers to stay home with their children, researchers did a study comparing children whose mothers stayed home and children whose mothers worked outside the home. Here's how the study was done. There were three groups of mothers with children. The first group, called "stay-home mothers," didn't work outside the home during their babies' first three years. The second group, called "home-then-work mothers," stayed home the first year and then worked the second and third years. The last group, called "working mothers," worked all three years after their babies were born. The reasearchers designed their

This article is continued on the next page.

A Model Teacher-led Discussion

study to answer this question: How were children affected when their mothers worked? To find this out, the children of these mothers were given intelligence tests after each year.

Which children do you think did the best on the intelligence tests: children of "stay-home mothers," children of "home-then-work mothers," or children of "working mothers"?

Here are the results: The researchers found that after the *first* year, the children whose mothers stayed home did the best. Put another way, the children of the "stay-home mothers" and "home-then-work mothers" did better than the children of "working mothers" at the end of the first year. However, after the *second* year, there were no differences among any of the groups. And finally, surprisingly, at the end of the *third* year, the children of the "working mothers" did better than the children of the "stay-home mothers"!

Many people were surprised to hear these results. This is how researchers explain them. They said the results show that it's very important to have good child care during the first year. The children of mothers who worked during the second and third years probably attended day-care centers or pre-school, so they had more contact with other people than if they had just stayed home with their mothers all day. The experts concluded that children benefit from having contact with other children and adults as they get older. Another probable explanation of the findings is that mothers who work often have more money to spend on books, computers, and educational toys for their children.

Instructions for Leading a Discussion

Format: Groups

Preparation Steps
(1) Get in groups of 2, 3, or 4 students.
(2) With your partners, choose one of the discussion topics listed on the next page, and tell your teacher your choice. Each group must choose a different topic, and each of you will lead a discussion on this topic.
(3) Go to the page with the reading you have chosen for your discussion and read the article. Help each other understand all the words. ***Don't read the other articles.***
(4) With your partners, write five *Factual Questions* about the article and eight to ten additional *Reaction Questions*.
(5) Practice reading the article.
(6) Your teacher will provide a schedule of when you'll serve as a group leader and when you'll be a discussion participant.

When you're the discussion group leader
You'll be a discussion group leader for about 40 minutes. (Each of your partners will be the leader of another group.)
(1) Read your article to your group and use lots of **discussion strategies** (e.g., ask them if they understand, answer their clarification questions and ask members to help you explain, explain words they don't understand, and ask members to help you explain).
(2) Ask the five *Factual Questions* you have written.
(3) Ask your *Reaction Questions*, and use **discussion strategies** (e.g., ask follow-up questions, ask for more details).

When you're a member of a discussion group
(1) Each discussion will be led by one person. Everyone else will participate as discussion group members.
(2) Try to be an active member by using **discussion strategies** (e.g., ask clarification questions, answer with details, ask other members follow-up questions, volunteer answers, clarify by summarizing, and help the leader explain).

Units 30-37 • For Students, continued

Choose one of these articles

Unit 30 Vacations Without Stress – *page 196*
An expert gives advice on how to plan a vacation.

Unit 31 Stronger Women – *page 197*
The role of women has been changing recently. This article tells about some of the changes.

Unit 32 Saving Uncommon Languages – *page 198*
This article tells about an island where there are 1,300 languages. However, soon nobody will be able to speak any of them, because international languages are beginning to dominate.

Unit 33 Culture and Alcoholism – *page 200*
People from several different countries talk about how alcohol and alcohol abuse are viewed in their countries.

Unit 34 Finding a Marriage Partner in a Foreign Culture – *page 202*
This article tells about people who live in a foreign country and want to find a partner to marry.

Unit 35 Siblings – *page 204*
This article explains why siblings, i.e. brothers and sisters, often fight with each other and why sibling relationships are important.

Unit 36 Rumors and Vampires – *page 206*
There was a rumor about a vampire that was attacking animals and people. This article explains how the rumor started and people's reaction to it.

Unit 37 International Students in the U.S. – *page 208*
Two international students tell about their experiences in a North American school.

Instructions for Leading a Discussion   • *195*

Format: Large Group/Whole Class

Vacations Without Stress

Most people take vacations in order to relax; unfortunately, vacations themselves can often become stressful. Experts have some advice to help people reduce this stress. First, we should try to take our vacations during the off-season or during the middle of a week. By doing this, we can avoid crowds so it will be more peaceful at beaches and parks. During off-season times, we will also have a better chance of getting hotel and restaurant reservations, and the prices at resorts and hotels are often cheaper.

Another way to reduce stress is to plan in advance, for example, by making reservations for hotels and popular restaurants. If we have a traveling partner, before starting our vacation, we should discuss with them our daily pace, in other words, how many things we want to do every day, and also how much money we expect to spend. It is best to plan only one big activity each day, and then decide later to do smaller things depending on how much time and energy we have. We should also plan some time every day to be quietly alone in order to relax.

It is suggested that we spend one vacation day at home before starting a trip, to get ready, and one vacation day at the end of our vacation to rest and prepare for the next day at school or work.

Factual Questions about the article

1. _____
2. _____
3. _____
4. _____
5. _____

Reaction Questions about your opinions and experiences
(You can write your own questions and/or choose some of these.)

· When you travel for a vacation, what's your main purpose?
    a) to relax   b) to see something new
    c) to meet new people   d) other
· If you were going to have a travel-vacation next week, who would you want to go with?
· Tell us about a vacation that was stressful for you.
· If I visit your country for a vacation, what would you recommend that I should do?

                                     Eight Discussion Choices

Format: Large Group/Whole Class

Stronger Women

Women nowadays are stronger and smarter than they were 50 years ago, and they can expect to live longer. Japanese women, for example, can expect to live 82 years, which is the longest in the world. Just 50 years ago, Japanese women could expect to live only 54 years.

Many women are working today. In Japan, 75% of women are working now, compared to 37% 50 years ago. The reason why so many women are working is that they're getting more education these days. The rate of Japanese women going to junior college and universities is higher than the rate for men.

In 1947, the average Japanese woman got married at the age of 23. Today, the average is 26. Divorce has increased by 50%.

As for having babies, today the birth rate is only 1.5 births for each woman. Fifty years ago, the birth rate was 4.5 babies.

In a recent survey, Japanese women were asked whether they would choose to be a man or a woman in a future life. 65% said they would prefer to be born again as a woman. In 1960, only 27% said they would want to be a woman again in the future. This suggests that nowadays more Japanese women are happier with their lives.

Factual Questions about the article

1. _____
2. _____
3. _____
4. _____
5. _____

Reaction Questions about your opinions and experiences

(You can write your own questions and/or choose some of these.)

• Who do you think is stronger, your mother or your father?
• Why do you think the divorce rate is increasing in some countries?
• What are the advantages and disadvantages of having children?
• Do people in your family live to an old age, such as 90 years old?

Format: Large Group/Whole Class

Saving Uncommon Languages

Do you know where New Guinea is? It's a big island near Australia. On this island, surprisingly, 1,300 different languages are spoken. Unfortunately, almost all the languages are about to become extinct. In other words, soon there will be no living speakers of these languages.

The reason there are so many languages is that New Guinea has many areas that are isolated because of mountains, rivers, and the sea, so the people in these areas have little contact with other people. For example, there will be a language spoken by the people on one side of a mountain, and on the other side of the mountain the language will be totally different. In fact, these neighboring languages can be as different from each other as Spanish is from Japanese.

There are some interesting things about these languages in New Guinea. One apparently has a vocabulary of only a few hundred basic words. This is probably because the people have a very simple life. Another language has a name for each bird and animal according to the sound the animal makes; for example, they call a dog "rrrufff" because for them that's the sound of a dog's bark. Another interesting language has a word for "stand" but no special word for "walk." If they want to say "walk," they must say "stand here and stand there." Another language has 36 names for bananas. It's also interesting that none of the languages in New Guinea has words for "thank you" or "hello." Isn't that amazing? And yet, by contrast, these languages have lots of words for nature and magic.

Many languages around the world are dying because of the spread of English and other more common languages. In fact, experts think that 90% of the languages in the world will disappear within the next 50 years. For many languages, one of the

Unit 32 is continued on the next page.

Eight Discussion Choices

reasons their use is declining is that there are no words for new technology, for example, for computers, so the speakers have to use English or another of the languages now spoken worldwide to talk about technology.

How do people try to preserve their uncommon languages? Many ways are being tried. For example, in order to keep the languages of New Guinea alive, the government wants the schools to use the local language in the first three grades of elementary school. Then, starting in 4th grade, the students can use English or another world language in their studies.

Factual Questions about the article

1. _____
2. _____
3. _____
4. _____
5. _____

Reaction Questions about your opinions and experiences
(You can write your own questions and/or choose some of these.)

• Besides English, what foreign language would you like to be able to speak?
• If you visit different parts of your country, do you sometimes have trouble understanding the people there?
• Tell me how teachers taught you English when you were younger?
• Do you think there's a problem because English is a common, international language?

Format: Large Group/Whole Class

Culture and Alcoholism

At a university in the U.S., some international students were asked to talk about the attitude toward alcohol in their cultures. The students who participated were from France, Argentina, Japan, Russia, and one Arab country.

According to the French student, the French drink a glass of wine with almost every meal. For her, alcohol is an everyday part of life, even from a young age. French parents teach their children about alcohol. They believe a glass of red wine every day is good for you. The French student also explained that people don't drink in order to get drunk, but rather, they drink to be sociable. Furthermore, they feel that drinking wine during meals helps them enjoy the taste of their food more. Because the French start drinking at an early age, they don't think of it as being an adult activity; therefore, most young people don't abuse alcohol. However, if someone develops a problem with alcohol in France, they can easily find a free clinic that will help them.

The woman from Argentina said that in her country also most people drink to be sociable. There are few traffic accidents as a result of alcohol, because most people feel a responsibility to be careful when they drink too much. For example, they usually walk or take a bus if they feel drunk.

The Japanese student said that Japan doesn't have very strict drinking laws. He said that it's easy for young people to get alcohol, so there are often problems with alcohol abuse. In Japan, alcohol is sold in vending machines; this means that even children can buy it! According to this student, there are many accidents in Japan caused by drunk drivers. One cause of the problem is that companies often organize drinking parties after work, so workers feel pressure to drink.

When asked about his country, the Russian student looked very sad. Drinking is a great problem in his country, he said softly,

Unit 33 is continued on the next page.

and nobody knows what to do about it. The government talks about solutions, but no one takes the talk seriously. This problem has deep roots in the culture and the history of Russia, the student added, and it will only change when great changes come to the life of the average Russian.

Finally, the Arab student talked about alcohol in her country. Since hers is a Muslim country, alcohol is strictly forbidden. Simply put, it's against the law to sell or drink alcohol, and it is against the religion. It is true that some people do buy alcohol on the black market. However, since most people obey the law, there's no problem with alcohol abuse.

Factual Questions about the article

1. _____
2. _____
3. _____
4. _____
5. _____

Reaction Questions about your opinions and experiences
(You can write your own questions and/or choose some of these.)

• Are the drinking customs in the U.S. and your country the same?
• What does alcohol mean to you?
    a) relaxation
    b) feeling happy
    c) celebration
    d) forget your problems
    e) a waste of time and money
    f) something unhealthy
    g) something evil
    h) other
• Some teenagers in the U.S. drink alcohol because they want to be like adults. Do teenagers in your country do things to be like adults?

Format: **Large Group/Whole Class**

Finding a Marriage Partner in a Foreign Culture

Koreans are the largest foreign minority in Japan. One of these Koreans living in Japan is a young woman named Ko, and another is a young man named Shin. Ko lived in South Korea until she was in high school, when she moved to Japan with her parents. At home in Tokyo, she continued to eat traditional Korean food and to follow Korean customs. Naturally, even today she feels like a foreigner in Japan.

On the other hand, Shin has lived his whole life in Japan, even though his parents are Korean. He feels like he is a Japanese, and actually he feels like a foreigner when he visits Korea!

When Ko and Shin were in their early 20s, they started to consider the idea of getting married. Ko never thought of marrying a Japanese man, because she considers herself a Korean. She felt it would be uncomfortable for her to marry a non-Korean man, because her family is very close and they celebrate important Korean religious events in their home every month. Her parents told her to marry a Korean. As for Shin, he considered marrying a Japanese woman since he felt so comfortable with Japanese customs and lifestyle, although Shin's parents also wanted him to marry a Korean.

As a matter of fact, in Japan, it's very difficult for young Korean people to meet other Koreans, so a certain Korean woman living in Tokyo started a club which held parties where young Koreans could meet. The purpose was to encourage Koreans to marry other Koreans, in order to preserve their traditions. At these parties, there are usually 20 people in their late 20s and early 30s. They eat dinner together, introduce themselves, and talk

Unit 34 is continued on the next page.

together. Sometimes, during the party, everyone changes seats in order to meet as many new people as possible. Ko and Shin met each other for the first time at one of these parties and got married six months later.

For Ko, it was very important that she had a chance to meet Korean men. She said it would be impossible for her to fall in love with someone, unless she felt comfortable with his ethnic background.

Among Koreans living in Japan, only 20% of the Korean parents said that they would allow their children to marry a non-Korean. However, times are changing. 50% of the Korean children said that marrying a non-Korean is acceptable.

Factual Questions about the article

1. _____
2. _____
3. _____
4. _____
5. _____

Reaction Questions about your opinions and experiences
(You can write your own questions and/or choose some of these.)

• Do you feel pressure (from parents, friends, etc.) to get married?
• Would you consider marrying someone from a different ethnic group or nationality?
• What are some things that would be benefits or difficulties for you if you married a foreigner?
• If you want to meet people your age, where do you go or what do you do?

Format: Large Group/Whole Class

Siblings

Some parents worry about siblings, in other words, brothers and sisters, who fight with each other. Some days, brothers and sisters get along fine with each other, and then suddenly they start fighting like enemies. It seems that they cannot spend time together without hitting or yelling at each other.

Specialists in children's behavior say that sibling fights are natural and that there are several reasons why they fight. For example, siblings need to show that they're different from their brothers and sisters. For this reason, siblings of the same sex will fight more often than siblings of the opposite sex. If the siblings are close in age, they'll fight more in order to show that they're different from each other. Also, when an older sibling starts junior high school or high school and doesn't want to spend time with a younger sibling, they might fight more.

Another reason why siblings fight is jealousy. One of them feels their parents like the other sibling more. When siblings feel their parents don't treat them fairly or equally, they tend to fight with each other. Often a child in this situation will actually be angry at the parents, not the brother or sister, but it's easier to show anger at a sibling than at a parent.

Actually, sibling fights can have some benefits. Children can learn how to get along with others. If they're having a problem with someone, they need to learn how to solve the problem without fighting. Kids get a lot of practice with their siblings in solving "people problems."

Parents sometimes worry because it seems their children's fighting is serious and almost dangerous. However, psychologists say that siblings rarely hurt each other. Usually, kids are noisy

Unit 32 is continued on the next page.

Eight Discussion Choices

when they fight, because they want to get their parents' attention. When the parents aren't around, the fighting usually stops. Parents should be more worried if their child is fighting with other children outside the family.

Usually, when siblings become teenagers, they don't fight as often. One reason is that siblings learn that if they work together "as a team," they can often convince their parents to give them special treats. For example, if they want to buy a video or go to a special concert, they learn that if they talk to their parents together, the parents will often agree.

Factual Questions about the article

1. _____
2. _____
3. _____
4. _____
5. _____

Reaction Questions about your opinions and experiences
(You can write your own questions and/or choose some of these.)

- Do you think your siblings had an influence on you?
- Do any of your siblings get more attention from your parents than the other siblings?
- How do you feel about your position in your family (e.g., oldest, youngest, middle, or only child)?
- If you have children someday, will you raise them the same way your parents raised you?

Format: Large Group/Whole Class

Rumors and Vampires

In Mexico, one day, a farmer said he had seen a giant animal or vampire that looked like a bat flying over his farm. Later he found 24 of his sheep dead. They had bite marks on their necks and all the blood had been sucked from their bodies. Soon a Mexican TV station came to investigate this story because there had been other, similar vampire reports. Soon after the TV report was aired, more reports came out about the giant blood sucker. Any time there was a death of a chicken, goat, or sheep, it was blamed on this vampire. Other people blamed it on a monster from another planet.

People were afraid. Mothers began keeping their children home from school. Farmers, who used to start work at 4 a.m. so they could finish before the afternoon heat, waited until after the sun rose before going to their fields.

The government conducted an investigation by studying some of the dead animals. They found that the sheep had been killed by coyotes, wild dogs, or wolves. The government reported the results and told people to remain calm. Nevertheless, many people were still willing to believe in the blood-sucking vampire.

Many people said they had seen the vampire. It was blamed for attacking animals and even humans. One farmer even said that it looked like a meter-tall dinosaur with huge teeth, large eyes and bat wings.

Finally investigators discovered how the vampire rumor had started. One day, a girl fell down some stairs in her house. She was lying at the bottom of the stairs, the bone in her arm had come out, and she was screaming, "Mama, I fell!" But the mother thought she heard her daughter say, "Mama, animal!" The mother ran to the neighbors to tell them that an animal had attacked her daughter. The neighbors ran into the house and saw the girl's bloody arm. At that moment, a group of black birds

Unit 32 is continued on the next page.

Eight Discussion Choices

flew away outside the house. Because it was getting dark outside, to the neighbors the flock of birds looked like a giant bat flying. That is how the rumor started in this small town.

In order to stop this fear, more investigations were done. It was determined that every dead chicken or sheep had been killed by a coyote, wild dog, wolf, panther, or some other wild animal. Because of a recent drought in that part of Mexico, these preditors were hungry and were killing livestock. In several towns where the people had seen the most vampires, the investigators even did some experiments. At night, they put sheep in a pen and secretly watched them. Late at night, some wild dogs came and attacked. The investigators found the same marks on these sheep as were on the original sheep which had been killed by "the vampire."

Belief in the vampire continued to break down when a man who said he had been attacked by it admitted that he had been hurt in a drunken fight at a bar. Even today, although the government reported all these results, some people still believe that there is a vampire in that little Mexican town. Vampires are notoriously hard to kill.

Factual Questions about the article

1. _____
2. _____
3. _____
4. _____
5. _____

Reaction Questions about your opinions and experiences
(You can write your own questions and/or choose some of these.)

• If this story happened in your hometown, what would you do?
• Do some people in your country believe in vampires, ghosts, or monsters?
• Tell me about a rumor that spread in your country, city, or school.
• Tell me about time when you were very frightened.

Format: Large Group/Whole Class

International Students in the U.S.

Two 17-year-olds discussed their experiences as international students in the U.S. The students, from Brazil and France, had studied at a high school in Wisconsin.

Poliana came from Brazil to the U.S. for academic reasons. She wanted to improve her English, because it could help her get a better job, maybe even a job teaching English someday. She's interested in traveling and studying different cultures. She said that Brazilians try to copy North American customs, so she was interested in understanding why.

Before coming to the U.S., Poliana had a certain image of North Americans. She got her image of North Americans from watching North American TV and movies in Brazil. She saw several Hollywood movies about high schools in the U.S., and she imagined high school could be a lot of fun. High school students seemed to have a lot of freedom. She imagined they participated in a lot of fun activities both inside and outside ofschool. However, she now thinks that Brazilian students have more fun and freedom in school.

Poliana sometimes feels disappointed because outside of school there are few places for young people to meet their friends and talk. In Brazil, young people often get together at parties or at a shopping mall.

In addition, Poliana thinks most North American students pretend to like her, because she comes from a foreign country, but actually don't make an effort to get to know her well. She also feels North American students often discriminate against other students who don't have fashionable clothes and hairstyles. In her opinion, North Americans aren't open to different cultures and customs.

On the other hand, Poliana says she likes North American ice cream, horses, and fashions.

The second student, Caroline, comes from France. The things she likes the most about North America are her host family, cheeseburgers, and peanut butter.

Unit 32 is continued on the next page.

Eight Discussion Choices

Like Poliana, before coming to North America, Caroline had some images of what she expected. She imagined that there would be a lot of freedom and that North America would have many things that she couldn't find in France. She believed in a stereotype. She was sure North Americans would all be wonderful, attractive, and very intelligent. After arriving, she found out she'd been wrong. And, unfortunately, to make matters worse, many North Americans seemed uncomfortable with her when they found out that she was French.

Caroline has noticed two big differences between North American and French young people. First, she thinks it's strange that people under 21 can't drink alcohol, as they can in France. And second, it seems all U.S. teenagers dress in the same style of clothes. In France, there's a greater variety of fashions.

These were the observations that two international students made about their experiences living and going to school in a small North American town.

Factual Questions about the article

1. _____

2. _____

3. _____

4. _____

5. _____

Reaction Questions about your opinions and experiences
(You can write your own questions and/or choose some of these.)

• Before you met any Americans, what image did you have of them? Did your image change after you met some?
• Have you visited any other countries? Were the countries or people different from what you had imagined before going?
• What three countries would you like to live in for a year?
• In general, how do people in your country treat foreigners who visit or live there?

Format: Large Group/Whole Class

Students' Choice
Designing and Leading Discussions

Preparation steps

(1) Find an article that you think would be interesting for the other students in the class. The article can be in your native language or in English.

(2) Tell your teacher the general topic of the article. Each student should have a different article and topic.

(3) Write a summary of the main idea of your article with some interesting details. This will be the basis for the discussion.

(4) Write *Factual Questions* about the article and some *Reaction Questions* asking about your partners' opinions and experiences.

(5) Your teacher will schedule you to be the leader of a discussion and tell you if you will lead a whole-class or a large-group discussion. Your teacher will set the discussion time for 20, 30, or 40 minutes.

When you're the discussion leader

1. Give your summary to the group and use **discussion strategies** (e.g., ask them if they understand, answer their clarification questions, explain words they do not understand, and ask other participants to help you explain ideas.)

2. Ask your *Factual Questions.*

3. Ask your *Reaction Questions,* and use **discussion strategies** (e.g., ask follow-up questions, and ask for more details.)

When you're a member of a discussion group

Try to be an active member by using **discussion strategies** (e.g., ask clarification questions, answer with details, ask other participants follow-up questions, volunteer answers, clarify by summarizing, and help the leader explain words and ideas.)

Suggestions to the Teacher

General

Why these activities were developed

A complaint often heard from both ESOL and subject-matter instructors is that their international students are passive in group and whole-class discussions. At the same time, international students tell us that they're quiet because they feel they don't know what to say, they don't feel they have anything interesting to say, or they have difficulty understanding what others say but are embarassed to admit it. Furthermore, they may say they come from cultures where spontaneous give-and-take interaction in class isn't valued (or is even discouraged), and they don't know the "rules" for participating in this kind of of interaction. This text is designed to better prepare international students to interact in discussions.

The approach and sequence

The units are presented with detailed instructions, so that the role of the teacher, after getting the students started, becomes that of supporter and coach. The students develop their skills and confidence by practicing with each other. The sequence of units leads from relatively easy challenges to the ultimate goal of leading and participating in a large group discussion, and therefore, as the later units build on earlier ones, the units are intended to be done in the order presented.

It should also be noted that the group format for the units leads, in general, from pair and triad work to large group and whole-class work. This approach is another reason for following the units in order.

In the event that your class doesn't divide easily into pairs or triads, two students can work together as a team carrying out the "Student A" role. For example, let's say you have 20 students and the unit calls for triads. You set up six groups of three, and then have each of the remaining two students team up with one of the students who has been assigned the role of "Student A."

Suggestions continued

Setting up discussion groups

There are various ways to form the pairs, triads, and groups. Some teachers may feel most comfortable taking on the role of match-maker. With specific classes, depending on the mix of personalities or other cultural considerations, it may be important to assign students to groups carefully, with an eye toward balancing the challenge and comfort that each student needs. An extremely shy and hesitant student probably should not be assigned to a triad with two other students who are aggressively eager to express themselves. When getting started with this book, some match-making should be considered if the style of these discussion activities is new to the students. Initially working in comfortable groups will help all the students gain confidence quickly.

On the other hand, random matching can easily be justified, since the activities are designed to turn taciturn students into active participants and talkative dominators into willing turn-takers. Another benefit of random matching is that the reorganizing and rearranging of groups, day after day, creates situations in which the students, in fact, need to draw upon the various strategies introduced in the text to interact with partners of varied personalities and abilities. Thus, by the end of the course, students will be experienced at working with other students who are more extroverted and more introverted, as well as others more and less fluent than themselves.

Getting started

Especially with Unit One, and even with some of the later units, it is important to be sure the students understand how the units are structured. Therefore, it can be helpful to choose a Student A and B team and walk them through the directions as the others observe, to show everyone how the activity works.

Students should be told to focus their attention on their assigned roles as Student A or B, etc., and not look at their partners' pages. "Cheating" spoils both the discussion and the fun.

Suggestions to the Teacher

Extending the activities

After some groups have (almost) finished the activity, ask everyone to stop. At this point, if there is time and the students seem involved and willing to extend the activity, you can invent ways of extending it. Here are two recommended options. You can ask everyone to switch parts, form new groups, and start over with just the *Reaction Question* discussions. Having changed the composition of the groups should make it more interesting to go back over the *Reaction Questions*. Or you can have the students discuss the *Reaction Questions* as a whole class.

Evaluating

Another important role that you as the teacher could play is as facilitator when the students evaluate their own and their group's performance and progress. The class as a whole can spend the final five minutes of class on "discussing the discussion." You may want to supplement this by providing individual students with some on-going feedback.

On page 217, following the notes on specific units, there is an evaluation form. How you use it is up to you. You could fill one out for each student, although this is difficult since you have several discussions going at once. You could focus on one or two students each day and give them a filled-out form as the basis for a brief one-on-one feedback session. Alternatively, you could have the students use the form for a self-evaluation or to evaluate their partners. Evaluations can be made after a certain number of classes or after specific units; the discussions in Units 6, 10 or 11, 14, 17, 21, 24, and 28, which summarize preceding lessons, offer appropriate occasions for evaluation. Whatever form or format you use, it is important to help the students assess themselves on an on-going basis, so that they see their own skill development and progress, two important aspects of developing confidence and expertise.

Dealing with early finishers

If you find that a group has finished the activity far in advance of the others, they could be offered three choices: a. switch parts and rediscuss the *Reaction Questions*, b. discuss any topic they like in English, or c. just take a rest and say nothing.

Suggestions continued

Special notes on specific units

Unit 1 and all of the following units provide your students with questions that are intended to stimulate discussion. Many of the questions ask students to share their personal opinions and experiences. This makes even the controlled discussions "real." However, a student may not be able to answer a question because it assumes they have had an experience they haven't had. This problem may embarrass them and make the whole discussion awkward for everyone. You may anticipate this problem by teaching the class this strategy. "What do you say if a question doesn't apply? Politely say you don't know or can't say, and give some explanation. For example: *A: Do you have to work hard in college? B: I'm sorry, I don't know. I'm still in high school.*"

Unit 3 is the first unit to use the news article topics, and for that reason, you may want to be sure that the students understand that they are to read the articles carefully enough so that they can discuss them in detail. Inevitably, they will encounter new words as they read; although vocabulary development is not the focus for this material, it may be important to allow them time enough to look up definitions or ask for help so that they will feel confident enough to discuss the topic. At any rate, you should provide some guidance on understanding the passage.

Unit 6 is the first "discussion unit," so you may want to be sure the students understand the purpose of the unit. In this case, as with later discussion units, they should attempt to put into use the strategies they have been practicing in the preceding units. In Unit 6, for example, they should be making a conscious effort to use the strategies of Units 1-5: rejoinders, asking follow-up questions, asking for clarification, providing comprehension checks, and answering with details.

Unit 16 has a unique set of directions involving a "small group" of five students. (If necessary, the groups can be four or six students.) Once again, be sure that the groups understand the directions for the activity. You may want to choose one team of five to "walk through" the directions while others observe how the activity works.

Unit 28 is a special summary unit in which all the strategies are reviewed and practiced. This unit includes a list of performance indicators, so it can be used to evaluate the students' progress in learning the basic discussion strategies. Videotaping one or more of the triads could provide a useful follow-up to this summary unit.

Unit 29 is a teacher-led unit, although you could have one or two of the more confident students take on the leadership role. This is the first "large group/whole class" unit, so if you model the role of the leader, the students can focus on participating as members, while at the same time observing your style as a whole class discussion leader.

Units 30-37 are large group/whole class discussions, in which the students have the opportunity to lead a discussion on their own. Although you could let the students choose which discussion topic they prefer, please note that the readings in these units progress in length with Unit 30 being the shortest. Keeping this in mind, you may want to assign the shorter passages to students who work more slowly and the longer ones to those who work quickly or who want more challenge.

The teacher's role

Throughout the book, once students have begun a unit there is usually little need for further teacher input. However, an effective use of your time is to roam among the groups, listening to the discussions and noting those who are doing well and those who are not. This information can allow you to provide additional guidance, support, and encouragement when they are needed and recognition and praise when they are warranted.

Note: On the next page there is a form that can be used for giving each student an individual evaluation. It is photocopyable.

Name _____
Date _____
Unit(s) _____

Discussion Evaluation

I heard you: **I didn't hear you:**

_____   Use rejoinders   _____

_____   Ask follow-up questions   _____

_____   Ask for clarification   _____

_____   Use comprehension checks   _____

_____   Answer with details   _____

_____   Interrupt someone appropriately   _____

_____   Re-tell information   _____

_____   Volunteer an answer   _____

_____   Re-tell others' opinions   _____

_____   Help the leader   _____

_____   Express an opinion   _____

_____   Refer to a source   _____

As a discussion leader:

You seemed to be _____ prepared.
   a) very well   b) well   c) somewhat   d) not

You _____ tried to get all the members to speak.
   a) often   b) sometimes   c) rarely

You _____ explained well if a member didn't understand.
   a) often   b) sometimes   c) rarely

You _____ asked follow-up questions about members' answers.
   a) often   b) sometimes   c) rarely

I think you should work on _____.

Resources for Developing Conversation Skills

Conversation Strategies: Pair and Group Activities for Developing Communicative Competence, by David Kehe and Peggy Dustin Kehe with illustrations by Andrew Toos. **This is the companion to *Discussion Strategies*** for students at the intermediate proficiency level. A student text with 24 activities giving practice with the words, phrases, and conventions used to maintain effective control of conversations. Strategies include polite forms, correction, agreement and disagreement, summarization, clarifications, follow-up questions, interruptions, and avoiding conversation killers.

Conversation Inspirations: Over 2000 Conversation Topics, by Nancy Zelman. 8 different conversation class activities: talks, interviews, role plays, chain stories and other group activities, and discussions. Procedures for each are clearly laid out. These include topic cards, monitoring, and correction techniques, and a variety of game rituals that make the conversation class effective as well as enjoyable. Inexpensive, quick and easy to use; *photocopyable.*

Cue Cards: Nations of the World, by Raymond C. Clark and Anna Mussman. For use in *role playing,* this is a set of 42 Cue Cards with detailed information about the most populous nations of the world. *Photocopyable masters.*

Cue Cards: Famous Women of the 20th Century, by Lisa F. DeWitt. For use in *role playing,* a collection of Cue Cards featuring 40 bio-sketches of women from 18 countries who have shaped or are shaping the world we live in. *Photocopyable masters.*

The Interactive Tutorial: An Activity Parade: 57 Activities for the Adult ESL/EFL Student, by Karen M. Sanders. Speaking, reading, and writing skills developed. Organized by communicative task, 12 topical themes, adaptable for younger students or small classes. *Photocopyable masters.*

Resources for Developing Conversation Skills

Index Card Games for ESL, edited by Raymond C. Clark. 6 game techniques for developing vocabulary, sentence/paragraph structure, pronunciation and spelling, questioning, and conversation skills through student-centered conversation activities. A "starter kit" of sample games at the elementary, intermediate, and advanced levels is given after each explanation. *Also available in French and Spanish.*

More Index Card Games and Activities for English, by Raymond C. Clark. 9 new language learning games using 3x5 index cards. The focus of these activities is on conversation skill building. The format includes explanations of the game techniques and a "starter kit" of sample games at various proficiency levels. *The samples may be photocopied.*

Play 'n Talk: Communicative Games for Elementary and Middle School ESL/EFL, by Gordana Petricic. 61 games to help children build conversation fluency and vocabulary, grammar and writing skills. *45 photocopyable masters.*

Solo, Duo, Trio: 128 Puzzles and Games for Building English Language Skills, by Richard Yorkey. For individuals, pairs, triads, and small groups. Working together promotes lively, constructive conversation. *Photocopyable masters.*

Lexicarry, by Patrick R. Moran. Students develop vocabulary by discussing drawings that illustrate functional language (greetings, condolence, invitations), sequences of actions (lose, look for, find), related actions (walk, run, skip), vocabulary topics (tools, color, clothing, sounds), operations (changing a light bulb), and places (office, living room, airport, and street).

Operations in English: 55 Natural and Logical Sequences for Language Acquisition, by Gayle Nelson and Thomas Winters. Often humorous classroom activities in which students working in pairs communicate naturally and accurately to accomplish set tasks step by step.

Resources for Developing Conversation Skills

Stranger in Town, by Lou Spaventa. A play for classroom performance and/or listening and discussion. A culturally rich and provocative story. High school to adult intermediates.

Story Cards: North American Indian Tales, compiled by Susannah J. Clark and illustrated in color by Ken Rainbow Cougar Edwards. Students choose one of the 48 illustrated Story Cards, read the story, and then tell it from memory to a partner or to the class. Each story can be the basis for fascinating intercultural discussions.

Story Cards: Aesop's Fables, compiled by Raymond C. Clark, illustrated in color by Hannah Bonner. 48 of Aesop's wonderful, classic stories, some well known and others not so familiar, can be used as the basis for many different conversation activities.

Story Cards: The Tales of Nasreddin Hodja, compiled by Raymond C. Clark, illustrated by Robert MacLean. These 40 stories about a funny and wise old Turk have been told and embellished by adults and children over the whole world touched by Islam for more than 700 years. The cards can be used for practicing story-telling and as the basis for many conversations on human nature and cultural comparisons.

Cultural Awareness Teaching Techniques, by Jan Gaston. 20 conversation activities designed to help students develop cultural awareness and sensitivity. Effective in any multi-cultural language classroom with students of at least intermediate language ability.

Related materials

Writing Inspirations: A Fundex of Individualized Writing Activities for English Language Practice, by Arlene Marcus. 170 writing-topic activity cards, containing hundreds of writing tasks *ready to be photocopied* and mounted on 5x8 index cards for students to choose from.

Resources for Developing Conversation Skills

The ESL Miscellany, by Raymond C. Clark, Patrick R. Moran, and Arthur A. Burrows. A compendium of information and vocabulary lists that will be the inspiration for many culture- and language-related conversations as well as many teacher-created lessons. *Fully photocopyable.*

Discovery Trail, by Mark Feder. 900 questions (90 in each of 10 areas - grammar, proverbs, idioms, geography and history, U.S. citizenship, etc.) are the basis for a board game or a quiz card game, either of which will stimulate hours of fun, varied conversation, and language learning.

Families: 10 Card Games for Language Learners, by Marjorie S. Fuchs, Jane Critchley, and Thomas Pyle. Students enjoy conversation, question and answer practice, and vocabulary building in any language using 40 humorous, full-color cards – 10 families each with a mother, father, daughter, and son. Each card has 8 features to ask about: clothes, hat, shoes, expression/emotions, object, money (numbers), transportation, and time.

The World: The 1990's from the Pages of a Real Small-town Daily Newspaper, edited by John N. Miller and Raymond C. Clark. 288 articles offer a wide-ranging selection of conversation topics from human interest stories to international sports and economics and science. Discussion topics are suggested for each article. There is a topical index. 6 teaching techniques are explained for use with any news article.

All of the above resources for developing conversation skills are available from **Pro Lingua Associates,**
15 Elm Street, Brattleboro, Vermont 05301 USA ✧ *800 366 4775*